The Bumper Book of Bravery

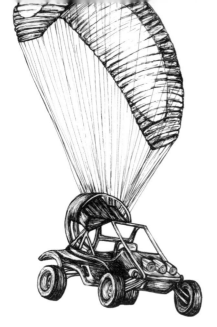

The Bumper Book of
BRAVERY

Charlie Norton

Published by Virgin Books 2009

2 4 6 8 10 9 7 5 3 1

Text design © Lindsay Nash
Illustrations © Nicole Heidaripour

First published in Great Britain in 2009 by
Virgin Books
Random House, 20 Vauxhall Bridge Road,
London SW1V 2SA

www.virginbooks.com
www.rbooks.co.uk

Addresses for companies within The Random House Group Limited can be found at:
www.randomhouse.co.uk/offices.htm

The Random House Group Limited Reg. No. 954009

A CIP catalogue record for this book is available from the British Library.

Hardback ISBN 9781905264834

Printed and bound in China by
C&C Offset Printing Co., Ltd.

For Rags MacGregor

Contents

Laying Down the Gauntlet 8

1. **War** 11
2. **High Seas** 35
3. **Aviation** 57
    Interlude – Samurai 81
4. **Survival** 99
5. **Espionage, Regimes & Revolutionaries** 123
6. **Exploration** 143
    Interlude – The Language of Bravery 167
7. **Sport** 183
8. **Escape** 207
9. **Death** 231
    Interlude – Noah's Own: Brave Animals 251

Read More About It 268
Acknowledgements 272

Laying Down the Gauntlet

Bravery comes in many forms. Some people are brave all their lives, some for a few minutes, some are brave for their beliefs, for humanity, and some are forced into situations where they draw from an unknown well of courage that has been lying latent within.

There are many different forms of bravery, of humans excelling under unbelievable stress or fear of pain or death or calamity – from the innocent strength of a child surviving the holocaust or a man walking alone across the Antarctic, to the innate bravery that surfaces when a person is forced to find extraordinary strength of mind just to survive. Bravery can be the sheer audacity of a sportsman's actions or the stoic will of a cancer patient who refuses to complain of the pain.

Man has dared to fly, to climb, to dive, to cure, to sail into the unknown, to fight tooth and nail for what he believes, to risk and sometimes sacrifice his life to save the lives of others. Man has sailed on 10-metre waves at over 30 knots, stormed hills with bullet-ridden bodies, and felt the exhilaration of freefalling thousands of metres and staying alive upon landing.

There are scientists whose courageous research has helped the future of humankind, there are politicians, diplomats and spies whose brave decisions have helped the greater good and there are sportsmen and -women whose performances have extended the boundaries of man's prowess. Such brave acts show how it is possible to evolve to be nobler, more knowledgeable and better adjusted to the world.

Some are eccentric pioneers, some are highly trained soldiers and some are ordinary people thrust into extraordinary circumstances. Some have professions which require them to risk their lives on a daily basis and some have had only extreme moments or split seconds where bravery has been required. Some do it for personal reasons and some for Queen and Country but many are brave for the other men around them, for their families or simply to survive and live a little longer. There are even animals who appear so strangely human when they suffer to save lives.

Different cultures have learnt to cope in different ways. Whether it's French individual brilliance, Russian teamwork, reckless American courage, British pluck, Spanish bravura, Brazilian flair, German thoroughness or the honourable death wish in the Japanese psyche, courage can be as much about knowing your absolute limit in the world, as it is about breaking through these natural confines. *The Bumper Book of Bravery* aims to cover a broad spectrum of human endeavour and seeks to show what mankind is capable of when treading the delicate balance required to proceed and to perform under extreme duress.

Everyone can feel small and vulnerable in battle, under torture or within the great folds of the earth; however, the very bravest acts are often made possible through an ability to control fear, to overcome a natural human emotion with an act of selfless dignity.

Such moments can be inspiring. When an explorer strains his ice-encrusted eyelids to see a towering mountain ahead or wipes his sweat-glazed eyes to see the folds of the desert shimmering, and remembers to savour the moment, the beauty of a savage landscape committed to memory, this is

when he must recall, as the French climber Lionel Terray said, that 'he knows the joy of rising for an instant above the state of crawling grubs'.

The bravery in this book tracks man's glorious struggle to overcome the impossible and to find where the invisible tightrope lies between glory and failure, camaraderie and egomania, good sense and insanity, and of course, life and death. But what must be remembered is that it comes from the humility of self-sacrifice, or utter brazenness and audacity, all of which helps us find our inner strength. Perhaps the twentieth-century writer who summed it up best was Ernest Hemingway when he said, 'Courage is grace under pressure'.

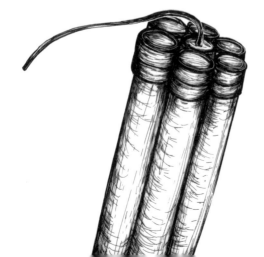

1 | War

A Whirlwind Five Years:
The War Cunning of Alexander the Great

The legendary commander of the Macedonians, Alexander the Great, amassed an empire in five years in the fourth century BC in a display of extraordinary courage and leadership. Five of his most important battles took place in less than five years. He was still in his twenties, had dark curly blond hair and dark blue eyes, and always led from the front in shining armour. He had a keen intellect, his endurance was invincible and his word was his bond. He was imitated by kings and military leaders throughout history. He was the first military genius.

335 BC *Battle with the Illyrians*

The Illyrians surrounded Alexander's army and lured them into a trap the Illyrians thought he would be unable to break out of. But Alexander loved a challenge. He thought for a while and then decided to parade his men before the enemy in total silence, moving their long spears up and down like a moving metal carapace. The Illyrians were bemused at what they were watching but a little fearful. Suddenly Alexander ordered his men to charge together at the centre of the Illyrian line while banging their swords against their shields as hard as they could and screaming the Macedonian war cry. In the ensuing chaos and confusion the Illyrians were routed.

334 BC *Battle of Granicus*

The great battle at the Granicus river in Asia Minor against the armies of the Persian Empire was the closest that Alexander came to death in battle. The Persian force stationed itself at the top of a steep bank on the opposite side of the river. Their plan was to concentrate their attack upon Alexander in the hope he might be killed, but Alexander led a successful wedge-shaped charge across the river and broke the Macedonian line, slaying several Persian nobles in the process. But one, named Spithridates, stunned Alexander momentarily by an axe blow to the head. Before the noble could deliver a death blow, though, he was himself killed by 'Black' Cleitus. Alexander recovered and his cavalry turned left and made it through to the weaker infantry and the Greek hoplites. They killed over 20,000 of the Persian army and, as legend has it, only lost a few hundred themselves.

Battle of Issus

333 BC

After invading northern Syria, Alexander left his wounded soldiers in a camp in the city of Issus, directing the remainder of his army south in search of Darius's Persian troops. In a maze of Syrian mountains, the two armies passed and missed each other, but Darius discovered the camp at Issus and massacred the wounded Macedonians. When Alexander returned he found Darius's army in a small area between the mountains and the ocean. The Persian cavalry was quickly surrounded by the Macedonian light troops and then Alexander led the charge, riding his horse Bucephalus directly at Darius, conspicuous in a golden chariot. Darius and his men panicked and fled.

Battle of Tyre

333–332 BC

This was the most protracted of Alexander's battles. It took Alexander seven months of laying siege to Tyre to hatch the right plan. Tyre was an island fortress off the coast of modern Lebanon. It was situated about half a mile off the mainland with the surrounding water approximately 5.5 metres deep.

To reach it from the Phoenician shore half a mile away, Alexander ordered the construction of a broad mole and

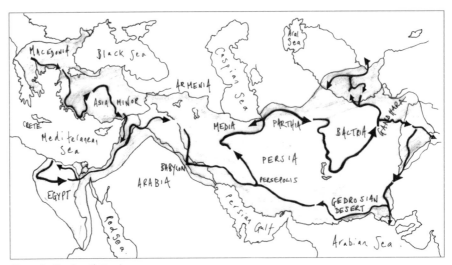

Alexander the Great's Empire

bridge guarded by towers. But the Tyrians bombarded his builders with stones and arrows, forcing Alexander to abort. He then mounted his siege engines and battering rams onto ships under huge tents to protect them. He pounded the walls until there was a small break, through which gangplanks led his men into fierce fighting in the city in July 332 BC. After killing 8,000 Tyrians Alexander had control of the eastern Mediterranean.

331 BC

Battle at Gaugamela

The Persian army assembled about 250,000 men on the plain of Gaugamela (now in Iraq) and, hoping to use a force of scythed chariots to break up the Macedonian army, Darius III had the plain levelled and cleared of all obstructions. By comparison, Alexander only had 47,000 men. He made a bold decision to attack the Persian left flank with his cavalry, another all-or-nothing move in which he adopted a formation in the shape of a hollow square, but heavily weighted with men towards the right wing. The Persians only thinned their formation, and Alexander immediately charged the weak spot in their line, breaking it in two. This quickly led to the final collapse of the Persian army. Darius III fled and the Persians retreated. The Persians lost tens of thousands of men in the battle, and the Macedonians lost fewer than 500.

On the afternoon of 11 June 323 BC, Alexander died in a palace in Babylon after drinking heavily at a banquet: he was either poisoned or sick. He was one month short of his thirty-third birthday. He had conquered most of the known world.

The World's Most Lethal Pony Club: Mongol Tactics at the Battle of Liegnitz

The extended pony club of Mongolian leader Genghis Khan was one of the most effective military armies ever assembled. Though the Mongols could be savage and barbaric in nature, time after time their skill in warfare allowed them to defeat much larger armies than themselves with a consummate ease that helped them establish the largest contiguous empire in history, one that covered at its greatest extent over 33,000,000 square kilometres. Their sheer professionalism was almost akin to that of a twenty-first-century army and their knowledge of battle tactics was second to none.

One of the most decisive battles on their western front was in 1241, when the Mongols faced Duke Henry II of Silesia outside Liegnitz (the Polish city of Legnica). The invaders from the east had already attacked Lublin and sacked Sandomir. Henry's army – which consisted of 30,000 Polish knights, Teutonic Knights, French Knights Templar and assorted infantry – was the last left to oppose them in Poland.

They faced 20,000 Mongols, fresh from victories over the other Polish armies and commanded by Kaidu, a great-grandson of Genghis Khan. For the Mongols, the battle served as a diversion to keep the European armies from uniting against them in their bid to conquer Hungary, which was the Mongols' primary aim.

When Henry reached the Wahlstadt plain not far from Liegnitz and surrounded by low hills, he found the Mongols already there, waiting for him. There was a huge gulf between the two armies – the knights in Henry's army were organised very hastily from different parts of the land, and even though they were disciplined and trained it was nigh on impossible to match the Mongol force, whose command was based on competence rather than birth, and who looked for victory at any cost.

The Mongols operated thousands of miles from home against opponents who outnumbered them. Their approach was to kill or defeat the enemy as efficiently as possible. Being so far away from their base, they could not afford to lose men or battles. They functioned in squads of 10, 100 and 1,000 that were highly responsive to commands signalled by flags during the battle.

The Knights Templar made a determined stand, but were killed to the last man without getting anywhere

The Mongol battle tactics were clever and allegedly infuriating. They were hunters who used speed, finesse and deception to herd their prey and kill them with minimal risk to themselves; in contrast, knights were prideful and looked for honour. The Mongols' protection lay in their cunning and they often wore no armour apart from an open metal helmet. The lumbering knights, complete with constricting chain mail, iron helmets, shields, lances and broad swords, would barely have been able to get near these fearless fighters.

Mongol methods of maintaining distance relied on the ability of their archers to shoot accurately, facing backwards while at a gallop on their Asiatic ponies. These ponies were their most effective weapon – each soldier had as many as three or four spare mounts. They were incredibly quick off the mark and could turn on a sixpence, much like modern-day polo ponies. They had superb speed and endurance compared to the encumbered war charger of a horse used by the knights.

Europeans were also unsettled by the lack of noise, as the Mongols operated without battle shrieks or trumpets; all signals were transmitted visually by flags, except for the strange whistling of certain arrows shot to incite terror and confusion in the enemy. To add further uncertainty, the Mongols appeared deliberately to be in very loose formations.

The first of Duke Henry's divisions charged into the Tartar ranks to begin close combat, but the lightly armoured Mongols easily surrounded them and showered them with arrows. A second charge by the remainder of the European cavalry seemed to be successful as the Mongol horsemen suddenly broke into a disorderly flight from the battlefield. But they had fallen victim to one of the oldest Mongol battle

tricks: the feigned retreat. The Mongol riders had been taught to retreat as a tactical move to draw the knights away from their infantry, after which they were surrounded by the nimble archers and picked off one by one. The unwieldy knights first had their horses shot out from under them, and then were slain by the lances of the Mongol heavy cavalry. The Knights Templar made a determined stand, but were killed to the last man without getting anywhere (rather like Monty Python's Black Knight, who fights on till the last while losing all his limbs).

The Mongols then cut the right ear off each fallen European in order to count the dead; they supposedly filled nine sacks. Henry was struck down and decapitated and the Mongols paraded his head before the town of Liegnitz on a spear. Most of Henry's army were also slaughtered. And although the Mongol casualties were heavier than usual, their victory proved why they were the toughest pony club in history.

The Battle of Gate Pa

Never has a British force which so greatly outnumbered the enemy been so heavily defeated. This extraordinary battle was fought on 29 April 1864, one of a number of heavy clashes in the Maori Wars (1860–72) fought between the native Maori and the British government which administered New Zealand as a colony. It also provided a story of serene heroism from a Maori woman, whose act is fondly commemorated in a church in England.

The governor of New Zealand, Sir George Grey, decided to send a force to blockade any reinforcements the Maori were trying to send through Tauranga on the east coast of the north island. He suspected this was a route open to the Maori from which they were trying to link up with fellow tribesmen in Waikato.

The Ngatirangi tribe, led by Rawiri Puhirake, had built a *pa* (a Maori fortification) not far from the British mission at Te Papa. It was a new style of hybrid fortification the Maori had learned to build to shelter from shells and muskets. The *pa* consisted of ten chambers excavated in the clay, communicating with each other: three at each side and two at each flank. Each chamber could contain 20 to 25 men. The 1,700 British troops did not quite know what they were taking on.

At daybreak on the morning of 29 April, in a powerful steady rain, the British, under the direction of General Cameron, began bombarding the *pa* with heavy artillery mortar and shell fire.

But the ingenuity of the trench and bunker kept the Maori well protected. During this bombardment, Rawiri strode up and down the parapets calling out to the gunners at each shot: 'Tena tena e mahi i to mahi' (meaning 'Keep up your work. Come on do your worst.')

But the bombardment, the heaviest of the Maori Wars, eventually created a breach in the right-hand corner. An assault party led by Colonel Booth (Forty-third Regiment) and Commander Hay (the Naval Brigade) took 300 men toward the breach at around 4 p.m. In a few minutes they were through the breach and inside the *pa*.

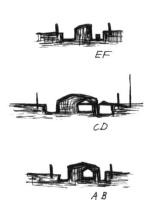

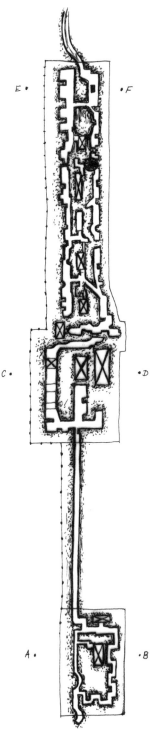

Plan of Gate Pa and cross sections

But the Maori had set a very clever trap. Their warriors pretended to retreat and then quickly concealed themselves in different parts of the underground chamber in trenches and rifle pits covered in branches and earth. The surrounding ground and pulpits were honeycombed with pits and secret passages. Rain during the day had turned the ground into a muddy bog. When the British assault party entered the main redoubt through a narrow gate, they did not know where to turn. As they slipped and flailed around, underfoot the Maori started close-range firing from an array of angles and concealed hideouts. As the hapless British soldiers were shot down in the mud, they panicked. They had nowhere to turn except back and the redoubt quickly became a killing field for the British soldiers and a turkey shoot for the Maori.

James Belich states in his book the *New Zealand Wars*:

> For one thing, the trap into which the British assault party fell was surely a remarkable tactical ploy. The use of concealed or deceptively weak-looking fortifications to ambush attackers was [...] a major element of the tactical repertoire made possible by the flexible modern pa. Rawiri's trap at Gate Pa was perhaps the ultimate refinement of this technique. It amounted to using the enemy's overwhelming strength against him and it involved the fearsome risk of allowing the assault-party, which alone outnumbered the garrison, into the main redoubt. Inside, the redoubt was less a fortification than a killing ground, as soldiers who inspected the redoubt after the battle attested. 'Those who were in this morning for the first time say that they never saw such a place in their life, and that you might as well drive a lot of men into a sheep pen and shoot them down as let them assault a place like that.'

The disorganised British fled back to their own lines, chased by the Maori from the main redoubt. It was a great victory for the Maori – 1,700 British soldiers repelled by 200 warriors. British losses were 38 men and 73 wounded while the Maori lost only 25.

Perhaps the most memorable moment of the battle of Gate Pa was the kindness of the Maori when the British soldiers lay dying through the night. Some of the Maori showed the true compassion and humanity of their tribe by giving water to the parched and wounded soldiers. One was a Maori woman named Heni Te Kirikaramu, who heard a dying man crying out for water and said to her brother, 'I am going to give that Pakeha [the Maori name for a non-Maori] water.'

So she sprang up from her trench while the fighting was still going on, found an old can full of water and ran towards him with bullets spraying all around. When she reached him he was rolling on his back and side in pain. So she lifted his head onto her knees and gave him water. He said 'God bless you.'

The soldier she helped was Colonel Booth, who died later that night. She then heard another wounded man crying out and then another who was trying to crawl towards the water. She gave them water as well and then left the water next to Booth before she made it back to her trench.

She was not forgotten by the British forces and there is a stained-glass window in the chapel of Lichfield Palace in England, commemorating her compassionate act of bravery.

Top Ten Most Ingenious Weapons

1. Zhuge-Nu Crossbow

For an effective weapon 'before its time', it is hard to beat the Chinese repeater crossbow. Attributed to the great Three Kingdoms-era strategist Zhuge Liang (AD 181–234), but possibly invented as far back as the Zhou dynasty (1000 BC) it is an extraordinary weapon. Though not always the most accurate or far-reaching, it could launch 10 arrows in 15 seconds, which, when it came to defending a fortified city or an army, was akin to firing a pre-industrial submachine gun. If laced with poison, just a nick could be fatal. They were used all the way through to the nineteenth century.

2. Trojan Horse

The Greeks spent ten years laying siege to Troy in Asia Minor after Trojan Prince Paris kidnapped Menelaus's wife Helen. In about 1188 BC, wily Odysseus, one of the Greek warriors, came up with the plan to leave them a gift outside the gates in the form of a gigantic wooden horse. The Trojans, spying no machinating Greeks about, were not, of course, wary of Greeks bearing gifts, so happily brought it inside the city walls. That night, as the Trojans lay sozzled with wine, the Greek warriors hidden inside crept out of the belly of the horse and razed Troy to the ground.

3. Blow Dart and Strawberry Poison Frog

One of the oldest, simplest and most lethal ways to kill with stealth is with the blow dart used to this day by the Amazonian Indians. The strawberry poison frog emits toxins that are among the most poisonous in nature. For this reason they have become known as 'poison dart' frogs to the Indians, who, knowing how to handle the deadly little blighters, carefully use them as an ingredient of curare to coat their darts.

4. Microdot

In 1870, during the Franco-Prussian War, Paris was besieged and a Parisian photographer named Dagron used a photographic shrinking technique that meant carrier pigeons could carry a high volume of messages on a tiny piece of film. This technology led to the modern microdot, which became indispensable in modern espionage as a method of secretly transporting large quantities of information.

5. Archimedes' Claw

This weapon was designed by the mathematical master Archimedes to defend the fortified harbour city of Syracuse from the Romans in 213 BC. Also known as 'the ship shaker', the claw consisted of a crane-like arm from which a large metal grappling hook was suspended. When the

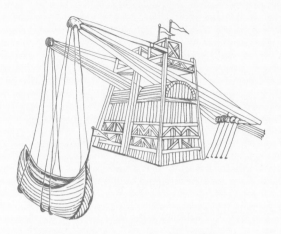

menacing claw was dropped onto an attacking ship the arm would swing upwards, lift the ship out of the water and possibly sink it.

6. RPG-7

The Russian rocket-propelled anti-tank grenade launcher is a particularly lethal modern weapon because it can easily be carried on the shoulder and used by one person. Delivered to the Soviet Army in 1961, it has a range of 500 metres and night sight and its simplicity, low cost and effectiveness has made it the most widely used anti-tank weapon in the world. It is used in guerrilla warfare everywhere.

7. Spy Suppositories

An ingenious place to hide your secret weapons is, of course, where the sun don't shine – in your nether regions. With a little awkward practice, everything from daggers, files (for escapes), tiny guns and wire cutters can be carried around inside special waterproof suppositories.

8. Lipstick Pistol

The lipstick pistol was issued to female Russian KGB agents in the 1960s. It was 4.5 millimetres long and known as the 'kiss of death', which was a little misleading as the chances were you never got a kiss before the lipstick got you.

9. The Exploding Cigar

Operation Mongoose – the name given to the CIA's covert operation to assassinate Fidel Castro with an exploding cigar – was the best known of the CIA plots to get rid of the Cuban communist leader. The idea was to get Castro to light a cigar packed with enough explosive that it would go off in his face, mortally wounding him. Of course it never worked and, judging by how many cigars Castro has smoked, it has never remotely worried him.

10. Poison Pen

The needle-firing pen was among the ingenious weapons designed by the British for Second World War undercover agents. A sharp needle could be fired at an enemy by pulling the cap back and releasing it. They were debilitating, not lethal.

Split Seconds of Bravery

Lance-Corporal Matthew Croucher, a Royal Marine commando, was on a covert, early-morning patrol to investigate a Taliban bomb factory when he walked through a tripwire that sent a grenade rolling out on the ground in front of him. Realising it would cover his three other comrades 'head to toe' in shrapnel the lance-corporal threw himself chest down onto the bomb. But a split second later he realised his injuries would be lessened if he took the blast in his back and rolled over.

He said: 'I was looking down and realised there was a grenade at my feet. I shouted to the other lads to take cover, grenade, and I lay down next to it to shield the rest of the lads from the blast. I had a horrible feeling like when I was a kid and I had done something very naughty. It was a terrible feeling of horror in my guts waiting for it to explode. But I would do it again.'

His citation for bravery noted that the action required 'extraordinary clarity of thought and remarkable composure'. The commando decided not to seek 'protection for himself but to attempt to shield the other members of his team from the impending explosion'.

Showing a 'complete disregard for his own safety' Lance-Corporal Croucher was 'quite prepared to make the ultimate sacrifice for his fellow Marines'.

By great fortune Croucher's Royal Marine-issue Osprey body armour and the contents of his backpack saved him from fatal injuries. He has received the George Cross for his spontaneous act of bravery.

Heroes of Telemark

One of the most daring missions of twentieth-century warfare was Operation Gunnerside, named by the British Special Operations Executive as the most successful act of sabotage in the Second World War.

British intelligence discovered that the German-controlled Ryukan hydroelectric plant at Vemork in Norway was turning out increasing amounts of deuterium oxide, or heavy water, a principal element needed to create nuclear reactions. The Allies, quite sensibly, feared that the Nazis might soon be ready to produce an atomic bomb. It was the only plant in the world capable of producing the quantities of heavy water sought by the Nazis, and, as such, was the most heavily defended structure in Nazi-occupied Europe.

Spring 1940

Operation Grouse: An advance party of four Norwegian Special Operations Executive (SOE) commandos, who had studied and memorised blueprints of the hydroelectric plant and surrounding area, were parachuted in for a reconnaissance mission. They were dropped into the wilderness over 100 kilometres from the plant and were given a couple of weeks to make the journey on skis.

18 October 1942

They eventually radioed the British, who asked, 'What did you see in the early morning?'

'Three pink elephants,' the Grouse team replied.

The mission was on.

Operation Freshman: This was a hastily planned, virtual suicide mission to land 34 British Royal Engineers in two

19 November 1942

Airspeed Horsa gliders on a frozen lake near the plant. The enthusiastic young men were sent without any way to get back apart from relying upon their own nous and a 400-kilometre trek without supplies, through unknown territory towards the safe haven of Sweden. The gliders were towed by Handley Halifax bombers – a hazardous flight made worse by the long distance from RAF Skitten in Caithness, disastrous weather conditions and terrible visibility.

One of the bombers crashed into a mountain, killing seven on board, and the glider cast off and crash-landed as well, killing several more commandos. The other Halifax could not find the landing site and decided to abort; however, the tow rope broke and the other glider also crashed, causing deaths and injuries.

The local Norwegians, performing feats of bravery themselves, organised a search and rescue, and trudged through waist-deep snow up a treacherous, rocky mountain, staying up through the night and most of the next day to help the survivors. Unfortunately, they turned the men over to the Gestapo, who they believed would treat them fairly as prisoners of war. What the locals could not have known was that, only days before, Hitler had issued a secret order instructing his troops to kill all captured commando personnel. The enthusiastic Gestapo based at Ryukan executed the order in this case without even taking the time to interrogate the prisoners first. These summary killings were later prosecuted as war crimes.

Operation Freshman failed and good men lost their lives without so much as a whiff of the hydro plant. The result was that the Germans were now alerted to Allied interest in their heavy-water production. Any new missions would be tougher.

The Norwegian Grouse team showed incredible mental tenacity in sub-zero temperatures during a long winter wait in their mountain hideaway. They endured four months of freezing hardship, subsisting on moss, lichen and a single reindeer that strayed past their camp.

British-trained Norwegian SOE commandos parachuted into the mountains 64 kilometres north of the hydro plant and were able to liaise with the reconnaissance party.

Operation Gunnerside: The commando force elected to descend into the ravine, ford the icy river and climb up the far side. The gorge, which the Germans considered impossible to scale, was left undefended. By skilful climbing and determination the commando team (the others were in radio contact with the British) made it 150 metres up the sheer rock face, during which they were completely vulnerable to attack.

With information from a Norwegian agent within the plant, they entered the main basement via a cable tunnel and through a window. All the men carried chloroform, ready to muffle any German guards as silently as possible.

Inside the plant the only person they came across was the Norwegian caretaker, who willingly cooperated.

With some standing guard and four carrying explosives, they split up to allow themselves a greater chance of success and managed to place explosive charges on the heavy-water electrolysis chambers and attach a fuse. All ran smoothly – in fact the only thing that really made the commandos freeze was when the caretaker said he'd misplaced his glasses and needed them back. For a few seconds they stood and looked at each other, wondering what on earth to do. The caretaker stressed that new glasses were nearly impossible to acquire in the war. There was a frantic search for his spectacles, which were eventually found.

The saboteurs deliberately left behind a British machine gun to show it was the work of British forces and not the local resistance with the aim of preventing reprisals against civilians. Finally the fuse was lit, allowing only a few minutes for escape. As they hared it out of the plant there was a dull thud behind them – a sign that the charges had detonated, destroying the electrolysis chambers.

They hid in the bushes and waited for the reaction, but only one German soldier emerged from the barracks and he soon went back in again, saving himself from being riddled with bullets. No one was killed during this raid.

All ten commandos made good their escape: six of them skied 400 kilometres to the Swedish border and four remained in Norway for further undercover work. The hydro plant was out of operation until April.

16 November 1943 The plant was attacked once more by a massive daylight bombing raid from 143 B-17 bombers that dropped a staggering 711 bombs over the area, 600 of which did not actually find the target. But they did quite enough damage to make the Germans stop and think.

20 February 1944 As a result of the bombing it was decided to move production to Germany. A ship was prepared to transport the heavy water across the nearby lake to get it out of Telemark. The British gave the immediate order to sink the ferry, even though there were local Norwegians on board. Many of them were known personally by the Norwegian resistance, who dutifully and unflinchingly followed orders and sank the ferry. Fourteen Norwegians died in the freezing water alongside the four German guards; however, the sinking halted the atomic programme completely. The Norwegian resistance involved in the factory sabotage and the sinking of the ferry are regarded as heroes, even by the families of those they had been obliged to kill.

Hardcore Yanks

Conqueror of Hill 543

Cornelius H Charlton helped prove beyond any doubt the fighting mettle and bravery of the African-American soldier while segregation was still thriving in the USA. There are few tales in modern warfare that would match his bravery near Chipo-ri in the Korean War.

Charlton was one of 17 children of a West Virginia coal miner who moved his family to the Bronx in New York City. Charlton enlisted in the army in 1946 at the age of 17 and served in Germany after the Second World War. Originally part of an engineering troop, he requested a transfer to the infantry and joined C Company of the Twenty-fourth Infantry Regiment, the last all-black unit known as the 'Buffalo Soldiers'. In a letter to his sister, sent in October 1950, he wrote, 'At last I am getting what I have been waiting for [combat duty].' It was signed: 'Love your bro, Cornelius.'

On 2 June 1951, near the village of Chipo-ri north of Seoul, his platoon encountered heavy resistance while attempting to take what was called Hill 543. Their platoon leader was wounded and evacuated by medics. A few days short of his twenty-second birthday, Sergeant Charlton suddenly assumed command, rallied the men and spearheaded the assault against the hill as though he was born for the role. Personally eliminating two hostile positions and killing six of the enemy with his rifle fire and grenades, Charlton continued up the slope until the unit suffered heavy casualties and became pinned down. But 'Connie', as he was called, knew no other way than forward. He regrouped the men and led them on, only to be hurled back by a shower of grenades.

Despite a severe chest wound, Sergeant Charlton point-blank refused medical attention and led an extraordinary third charge which somehow carried them to the crest of the ridge. He then noticed the remaining bunker on the reverse slope. He decided to charge it alone, was again hit by a grenade but raked the enemy position with a hail of bullets that eliminated its defenders. The terrible wounds received during his fearless exploits led to his speedy inevitable death. He was posthumously awarded the Purple Heart and the highest US accolade, the Medal of Honor.

Cornelius H Charlton made the ultimate sacrifice for his country while still barred from enjoying the same basic civil rights as his white compatriots and fellow soldiers; however, it wasn't until November 2008 that his family were granted permission to bury him at Arlington National Army Cemetery, where he rightfully belongs.

Navy-SEAL rescue

There are few elite special-forces units in the world to match the US Navy SEALs, and the stories we know of their bravery and self-sacrifice are only those that have been disclosed outside the top-secret restrictions that darkly shroud so much covert military operation.

When US forces were being withdrawn from Vietnam in the early 1970s, the 'unconventional warfare' role of Navy SEALs grew. The missions they undertook around the coast of Vietnam helped the SEALs realise their full potential. Their reputation as superhuman frogmen is summed up by this incredible story of blood and guts in October 1972:

Petty Officer Michael Thornton was assigned to a five-man reconnaissance mission under the command of Lieutenant Thomas Norris near the border with North Vietnam. Launched from a South Vietnamese Navy junk in a rubber boat at 5.30 a.m., the patrol swam to land from a mile out but soon realised they were not in the right place. It was a disastrous balls-up: the landing place was swarming with enemy NVA.

Thornton thought they must be further into North Vietnam because the enemy were making no attempt to disguise themselves: He said, 'We were under fire immediately, there were hundreds of them. You have to laugh or cry in that situation. Tommy laughed and said he reckoned he could handle 50 of them.

'I fell into a rhythm: shoot, roll over, shoot – always from a different position. I eliminated thirty-three enemy in the first half an hour.

'We tried to call in backup but there was no way in with all the Russian artillery fire of the NVA. They were certainly within ten yards of us just a dune away. A grenade came over and I must have thrown it back twice before it came back and exploded right beside me, giving me shrapnel wounds in my back.

'Then out of the blue the enemy started to fall back and retreat – we had killed a lot of them and they clearly did not know how many we were. We had been moving around so they could not pinpoint us and it had obviously worked.'

Kwai (one of the South Vietnamese in the party) made a dash for the shore and told Thornton that Norris was dead and it was no use. But Thornton would hear none of it and ran back like a man possessed into the gunfire.

'I ran back and when I found him he was unconscious, shot through the left temple out of his forehead and his eye and nose were gone,' Thornton said. 'I had to shoot a couple more enemy to get to him but he was still alive. I picked him up and put him on my back and ran.

I fell into a rhythm: shoot, roll over, shoot – always from a different position. I eliminated thirty-three enemy in the first half an hour.

'Sand was blowing up all around me and I was thinking are they bad shots or am I just one lucky son of a gun.'

Thornton had picked up Norris's AK-47 as he had already spent the ammo in his own weapon. He turned and walked backwards into the sea, firing as much as he could. He was shot through the calf and fell to the ground. But with the power of an ox he raised himself through the pain and waded into the sea, still carrying Norris.

'I was pushing us down through the surf so we were not such easy targets. Kwai had been shot in the hip, a buttock was gone and he was struggling in the water so I grabbed hold of him too. I managed to drag them both out to sea and keep them floating out of range of the fire from the shore – I reckon I got them about a mile out.'

After two hours they were picked up by the South Vietnamese Navy – and they all got out alive; however, as Thornton said, 'No one thought Tommy would make it and the first surgeon said no way. But there happened to be a top neurosurgeon out there too and he took him on. After a nineteen-and-a-half-hour operation he managed to stabilise Tommy.'

Then there were six more years of operations. Tommy Norris went on to become an undercover agent for the FBI for 22 years. As you would expect, he and Thornton have remained the firmest of friends.

2 | High Seas

Ming Admiral Cheng Ho

Not many people would associate China with feats on the high seas but it has not always been so. In the same way the Chinese invented gunpowder while the rest of us were still holding flints and wondering what to do with them, some of the oldest beginnings of great sea exploration originate from the hidden depths of the Orient.

More than a century before Europeans commissioned Da Gama, Columbus or Magellan to hoist their sails for the New World, the fourteenth-century Ming dynasty already boasted one of the most famous sailors of all time, Admiral Cheng Ho.

Cheng Ho was born in 1371 in Yunan, but after an invasion by the Ming dynasty in which his father was killed, he was castrated, as was the barbaric custom, and sent to serve at the court of the emperor as a eunuch. Cheng Ho became a trusted servant and eventually a military leader. By 1402 a contemporary said 'he walked like a tiger' and Emperor Yong'le

We traversed those savage waves as if we were treading a public thoroughfare

appointed him admiral and commissioned him to build a 'Treasure Fleet' to explore regions beyond China and its seas.

In three years Cheng Ho assembled the largest fleet ever to sail on the ocean. He had 62 ships, each 180 metres long, accompanied by hundreds of smaller vessels for his 28,000 entourage of crew including soldiers, navigators, doctors and scribes. A Chinese historian described the gathered vessels as 'houses that look like great clouds when they spread their sails'.

Cheng Ho went on seven great expeditions: to East Africa, Arabia, India, Indonesia and Siam (now Thailand). He sailed through hurricanes, a weather phenomenon he never knew existed, gained spiritual power in the eyes of the crew when divine light (probably the static electricity of St Elmo's fire) appeared to him, and he ruthlessly suppressed pirates who had long plagued Chinese and South-East Asian waters, capturing the famous Chinese pirate Chen Tsui.

Wherever he went he presented gifts of gold, silver, silk and porcelain. In return, China received such novelties as zebras, camels, ostriches, ivory and, most impressively, giraffes, since the Chinese thought they were some kind of long-necked, hybrid unicorns that would bestow wisdom. He brought trophies and envoys from more than 30 kingdoms. The records of Cheng's last two voyages, believed to be his farthest, were destroyed, which has led to speculation that he may have travelled as far as the Cape of Good Hope or even round the world. In 1420 the astute Venetian monk and cartographer Fra Mauro described a huge junk 3,200 kilometres into the Atlantic; however, this was more likely to have been an Arabian or European ship.

Zheng wrote of his travels:

> We have traversed more than 100,000 li [50,000 kilometres] of immense water spaces and have beheld in the ocean huge waves like mountains rising in the sky, and we have set eyes on barbarian regions far away hidden in a blue transparency of light vapours, while our sails, loftily unfurled like clouds day and night, continued their course as a star, traversing those savage waves as if we were treading a public thoroughfare.

Most historians agree that Cheng Ho died in 1433 on the return voyage of the seventh Treasure Fleet. After his death, China lost all braying rights on the high seas just before the golden age of exploration. She decided to concentrate on border enemies and turned inwards on herself at the cost of huge potential in international trade. She destroyed most of the nautical charts of Cheng Ho and decommissioned the treasure ships that sat in the harbours until they rotted away.

His achievements have since been recognised and the Chinese have a national holiday in his name.

Oldest Boats of War

Greek Trireme

As early as the seventh century BC, one of the first great warships appeared, the Greek trireme. At 35 metres long and 6 metres wide she had three tiers of oars (as opposed to a bireme, which had two). The top tier had 31 rowers on each side, the other two had 27 on each side. The crew of the trireme (excluding the 170 rowers on board) consisted of 20 sailors and 12 soldiers. Rowers gathered speed to 5 knots and when a sail was hoisted the speed reached 8 knots (14.8 kilometres per hour). The sail was used only in storms and during long voyages. At the moment of preparation for a battle the sails were furled and the masts lowered. Triremes often attacked other ships with their metal rams before fighting alongside hand to hand. They were fast and agile, and became

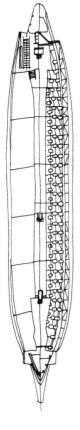

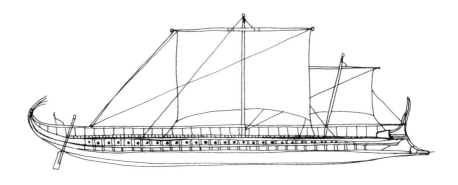

the dominant warship in the Mediterranean from the seventh to the fourth century BC. Triremes played a lethal role in the Persian Wars and the creation of the Athenian maritime empire.

Viking Longship

In the so-called 'dark ages' from around AD 500 to 1000 the Vikings may not have been as refined or educated as the Romans but they were able to do the seemingly impossible with their long boats. Danish Vikings attacked

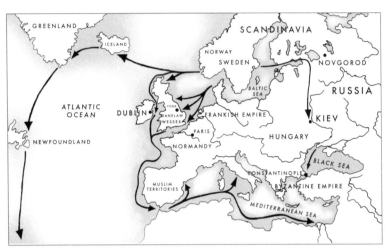

Viking exploration routes

England, France, Spain, North Africa and Italy and settled in Iceland, Greenland and North America. Swedish Vikings sailed up Russian rivers and even attacked Constantinople. They were insatiable – with all their outposts linked by the sea. A longship might be 40 metres long and only 3 metres wide. They were very narrow in relation to length, very speedy and manoeuvrable, and could be easily beached or rowed upriver. They were rowed by maybe 60 oarsmen and the 37-metre 'Long Serpent' built in AD 1000 for King Olaf Tryggvason of Norway could carry 200 men. The hull would have been flexible to ride over the waves and it would have reached around 4 knots under oars and 10 knots under sail.

Sea battle involved little manoeuvring; they just got alongside and fought hand to hand across the decks. On board there may have been a tent to keep the men from getting wet, but generally it would have been miserable sleeping on deck in the rough seas.

Ten Astonishing Facts

1. Longest Time Under Water in One Human Breath

Hungarian escape artist David Merlini broke the world record for the longest time under water without air in October 2007 in Hollywood. He was chained and handcuffed in a glass tank full of water for 10 minutes and 17 seconds.

2. Biggest Fish Caught

An 18-metre whale shark (*Rhincodon typus*) was caught in the Gulf of Thailand in 1919. The whale shark is the largest species of fish, and often grows to 13 metres long and can weigh up to 15 tons.

3. Largest Underwater Mountain

Mauna Kea on the Big Island of Hawaii rises 4,205 metres feet above sea level and a total of 10,203 metres from the Pacific Ocean floor.

4. Water Speed Record

Ken Warby in the *Spirit of Australia* managed to get to the incredible speed of 511 kilometres per hour at Blowering Dam in New South Wales in October 1978. With a fatality rate of over 85 per cent since 1940, the record is strictly for those with a death wish.

5. Biggest Wave Surfed

Ken Bradshaw surfed a wave over 24 metres high at Outer Log Cabins, Oahu, Hawaii on 28 January 1998. Ken's rogue wave was at about 11.30 a.m. – some video footage was shot from a mile away on shore documenting his 30-second ride.

6. Most Amazing Sea Discovery

In 1938 a fishing trawler operating off the tip of South Africa netted a very queer fish. Though it didn't look like it would be good with butter and lemon, the captain of the boat decided to take the 57 kilogram, 1.5-metre-long animal with bulging blue eyes and heavy bluish scales back to port. It turned out to be none other than a coelacanth, previously thought to be extinct for 65 million years.

7. Deepest-Ever Human Dive

Chief Navy Diver Daniel Jackson of the US Navy Reserve Deep Submergence Unit dived 610 metres in a newly developed hard suit in 2006 off the coast of Jolla, California.

8. Fastest Fish

The Indo-Pacific sailfish (*Istiophorus platypterus*) has been measured in excess of 109 kilometres per hour over short bursts. This fish grows up to 3.4 metres in length and 100 kilograms in weight.

9. World's Strongest Current

The Antarctic Circumpolar Current, which flows continuously around the globe, reaches down four kilometres to the ocean floor and transports about 100 times the volume of water of all the world's rivers put together.

10. Longest Ocean Swim

Australian Susie Maroney swam from Mexico to Cuba on 1 June 1998, covering 197 kilometres, the longest distance ever swum without flippers in open sea. It took 38 hours and 33 minutes.

Timeline: Tales of Circumnavigation

1519–22   *The Very First*

The first circumnavigation of the globe was a protracted affair led by the Portuguese Ferdinand Magellan. In 1519 he left Spain, which had helped with the finances, with five ships and 237 men, the majority of whom had not the foggiest idea where they were going. They might have mutinied or jumped overboard had they known that Magellan wanted to try to reach South-East Asia by sailing west across the Atlantic.

After finding the Magellan Straits, which then took his name, at the tip of South America, Magellan hit the Pacific, where his crew suffered unbearable hardship.

Antonio Pigafetta, one of the crew who kept a journal, wrote:

> We ate only old biscuit reduced to powder, and full of grubs, and stinking from the dirt which the rats had made on it when eating the good biscuit, and we drank water that was yellow and stinking. The men were so hungry that if any of them caught a rat, he could sell it for a high price to someone who would eat it.

Magellan himself was then killed in a fight in the Philippine island of Cebu. It was left to his second-in-command, Juan Sebastián Elcano, and seventeen other survivors including Pigafetta to complete the historic journey, returning almost unrecognisable as their former selves, half starved and in rags, in 1522.

1708–11   *Voyage of Privateer Captain Woodes Rogers*

This was a wildly audacious trip round the world in search of Spanish treasure and booty by the 29-year-old Bristol privateer Captain Woodes Rogers. It was mercenary raiding

with private investors' money in return for a share of the
booty, and sanctioned by the Navy on condition that he
confined his attacks to enemy vessels – legalised piracy in all
but name. Rogers's swashbuckling journey was a boy's own
tale of hardship, chaos, fighting, disease, starvation,
hurricanes and stamina. Life was cheap but booze and bounty
could be plentiful.

The *Duke* and her consort, the *Duchess*, ease down the Bristol   1 August
channel with over 50 guns between them, double-sheathed
hulls against worms, new rigging, six medical officers, flour,
salt, meat, beans, biscuits, grog, powder and ball.

On arriving at Cork, Ireland, 40 of the crew were immediately   12 August
lost into taverns and others married Irish biddies with careless
abandon.

With 150 new hands hired – 181 crew members in total on   1 September
the *Duke* and 153 on the *Duchess* – they set off from Cork on
the voyage.

Rogers lashes the coxswain Cash, who has already started to   12 September
encourage a band of mutineers. He puts ten of them in irons.
To avoid more trouble he sends Cash ashore at Madeira.

With Tenerife in sight, Rogers detains a Spanish barque full of   17 September
wine and brandy and holds the Spanish authorities to ransom
for 450 Spanish dollars and a longboat of wine, hogs and
grapes.

At the Cape Verde Islands Rogers says he will forgo his   8 October
captain's right to cabin plunder to help stop future mutiny by
the crew. One crew member dies falling overboard.

20 November	In a cove at Grande Island the investors' agent Vanbrugh shoots a musket at a suspicious-looking canoe and kills an innocent boatman transporting a friar.
3 December	They leave the Grande behind them, restock with limes, feed corn and liquor.
21 December	They come to the Falklands, an albatross in their wake, and coldwater porpoises abound. A crew member smashes his skull falling from the mizzen top.
6 January 1709	The two ships are buffeted by the rough seas like 'watery alps' around the Horn.
15 January	In the Southern Ocean, seven men die of scurvy and they set course for islands known as Juan Fernández, 640 kilometres away off the coast of Chile.
31 January	The ships arrive at Más a Tierra, the first island. When they go ashore they find a lone, barefoot man heavily bearded and covered in goatskins. His speech is muffled and broken. It is Alexander Selkirk, a Scot who has been there on his own for four years and four months – the original man on a desert island. He had with him his clothes and bedding, some powder, bullets and tobacco, a hatchet, a knife, a kettle, a Bible and books. This extraordinary find of Rogers, a friend of the author Daniel Defoe, was the inspiration for the character and book, *Robinson Crusoe*.
13 February	They set sail for Peru laden with goats from Juan Fernández.
25 February	Morale is finally boosted by their first prize on the seas: a 16-ton scrap vessel which Rogers called *The Beginning*.

Rogers captures two ships bloodlessly – the *Ascension*, a galleon of 450 tons with a load of timber, and a 35-ton coaster with £95 in coin and plate.

1 April

Two scouting pinnaces set out under Frye and Cooke to investigate a Spanish ship which immediately fires upon them. Two die and three are wounded from the enemy's first burst of fire. The younger brother of the captain, John Rogers, is hit on the skull and dies instantly. Later they capture the French-built boat *Havre de Grace*, renaming it the *Marquis*.

14 April

They storm the Peruvian port of Guayaquil successfully, but only after tortuous negotiations. The invaders prove more dangerous to themselves: one crew member is killed by case-shot exploding, a sentry shoots dead a fellow privateer after a misunderstanding over the password, one loses an arm on a grenade and Lieutenant Stretton's pistol goes off in his belt, shooting his leg.

21 April

After painstakingly ransoming the town for 22,000 pieces of eight and taking hostages, Rogers sets sail for the Galapagos. Most of the landing party go down with the plague and about 20 die of the ensuing fever.

8 May

At the Galapagos Islands, great for turtle and iguana meat, Rogers is attacked by a giant sea lion and has to stab it with a pikestaff. Thirty-two black slaves join the privateers as free men.

29 August

They hunt for prized Spanish galleons en route from the Philippines.

15 September

They attack Spanish galleon the *Encarnación* in the Pacific

20 December

and capture it. It is loaded with cloth, spices, jewels, plate and crucially, of course, wine, but Rogers receives a musket shot through his left cheek and cannot utter orders to his men. A number of the crew also have terrible wounds and are tended to by ship's surgeon James Wasse, who gags the men to stop them screaming as he cuts off arms and legs and uses boiling pitch to cauterise their wounds.

22 December A second Spanish galleon, the *Begona*, fights back with 12-pound guns and Rogers's ships are forced to retreat with holes all over them and many wounded.

10 January 1710 They anchor at Guam and a show of strength ensures supplies of corn, eggs, fowl, hogs and cattle.

10 May The crew are starting to fight starvation again – water is strictly rationed. Then they get lost around Asian islands – rats become a delicacy. Rogers is in much pain and grows thin and weak.

20 June They arrive at Batavia, which is run by allies the Dutch East India company, and spend four tedious months here. Rogers conducts a huge refit of the ships and the *Marquis* is sold for junk. A doctor pries the musket ball out of Rogers's jaw. Some men desert, some die of fever and one is bitten in two by a shark.

24 October They begin a slow run to Cape Town during which ship's surgeon James Wasse dies and Rogers can barely summon energy to write in his log.

29 December They arrive at Cape Town and spend three months waiting for convoy ships to transport them safely home with all cargo intact.

Twenty-five ships set sail, slowed by the Spanish galleon and the leaky *Duke*. They skirt Ireland to avoid French privateers in the Channel and ten Dutch warships take them in escort at the Shetlands.

5 April 1711

They anchor at Texel in Holland. Rogers finds out the English East India Company are taking legal action against him for trespassing on Asiatic waters.

23 July

Rogers's weary flotilla comes up the Thames to arrive at Erith. They are immediately set upon by gannet-like agents of the East India Company. Five years of legal battle ensue – the seamen receive no more than £50 each and Rogers gets £1,530, which is not enough to pay his bills and so he ends up bankrupt.

14 October

Up till then, only a few men had circled the globe; however, what made Rogers's feat even more remarkable than the others' was the fact that he brought his original ships home, including the prize galleon *Encarnación* (for others with better lawyers as it turned out) and he lost only about 50 men on the whole voyage.

Later, in 1717, Rogers was appointed governor of the Bahamas by King George I and played a major role in ridding the islands of close to 2,000 pirates, one of whom was Edward Teach, also known as Blackbeard, whom Rogers's men beheaded. On one occasion, Rogers hanged eight pirates in one day (although he spared a ninth at the last minute when he discovered his 'loyal and good' parents had come from Weymouth). His slogan 'Piracy expelled, commerce restored' remained the islands' own motto until independence was declared in 1973.

Great Moments of Bravery

Samantha Davies

Sam Davies, an English sailor beloved by the French, came an incredible fourth in the 2009 Vendée Globe solo round-the-world race on her boat *Roxy*. Not only was she the first woman in that particular race to reach the finish, but she also diverted her course during the race to help the Frenchman Yann Elies when he ran into trouble and broke his leg.

Sam says her greatest sailing moments were approaching Cape Horn, as strong winds, powerful currents, icebergs and crashing waves have made it notorious as a graveyard for sailors:

> The most defining moments sailing round the world were just before Cape Horn – I was facing 50-knot winds and waves of 8–10 metres in the Southern Ocean. It really focuses your mind. You know it's trouble when these waves are breaking over your boat. The sea bed shelves upwards out to sea and causes dangerously rough waters. And this was at the end of six weeks pushing as hard as I could.
>
> It all culminates at Cape Horn and I kept running on deck to make another manoeuvre. I had to change direction to keep the boat safe and lock down everything while the door was blown shut. Then *Roxy* got blown right on her side and the cockpit was flooded. But she came back up.
>
> It was so unpredictable I couldn't afford to sleep for 48 hours. In these wild conditions you have to live it moment by moment – I was right on the edge.
>
> But time came down slowly but surely and then I saw the rock of Cape Horn. I knew the worst was over.

U-47

Under the fearless command of Gunther Prien the German U-boat U-47 became famous for an outrageous feat of skill and bravery that caused much embarrassment to the British Navy at the outset of the Second World War.

Only two British battleships were sunk by German submarines during the whole of the conflict, one of which was lost in extraordinary circumstances in the Royal Navy base of Scapa Flow, under the very noses of the disbelieving British.

The mission into Scapa Flow was a very dangerous one. Located in the Orkney Islands north of Scotland, Scapa Flow was the main fleet anchorage of the Royal Navy and was regarded as an impregnable fortress, particularly against submarine attack. To undertake such a task was, in U-boat commander Dönitz's own words, 'the boldest of bold enterprises', for any prospective attacker had to deal with not only the heavy defences, but also the powerful and unpredictable currents. It was a steel nut to crack.

The 30-year-old Prien was a young self-confident Nazi – he had no hesitation in accepting the mission and predictably none of his crew left the sub when he gave them the chance.

On 14 October 1939 at dead of night, Prien risked

Route of U-47 in Scapa Flow

A Golden Age for France

The golden age of French circumnavigation is upon us. Centred on the Brittany coast around ports such as Sables d'Olonnes and La Foret, there is even a Pôle France Finistière academy for solo sailors. The sport appeals to the French penchant for high adventure, technical mastery and stretching the boundaries of individual courage. In recent times they have dominated round-the-world sailing, except for a brief interruption by Briton Ellen MacArthur, who broke the record in 2005.

1766–69: First French
The first French circumnavigation was by Louis de Bougainville on the *Boudeuse* and the *Etoile*. On board was Jeanne Baré, disguised as the male valet of botanist Philibert Commerçon. She was the first woman to circumnavigate the globe.

Records
1989 Olivier de Kersauson sets the fastest time for a solo multi-hull circumnavigation, taking 125 days in *Un Autre Regard*.

1990 Titouan Lamazou takes 109 days in *Ecureuil d'Aquitaine II*.

shallow water on the path through Kirk Sound, instructing his helmsman, Wilhelm Spahr, to take the narrow channel.

It was not long before they were holding their breath as *U-47* came within 15 metres of the block ship the *Numidian*, and was momentarily grounded on the exposed anchor cable of the *Seriano*. Astonishingly they were so close to the shore that they found themselves illuminated by the headlights of a passing taxi cab from St Mary's village.

But somehow no alarm was sounded and they found themselves in the main harbour at Scapa Flow. It transpired that the main British fleet had just gone to Norway on exercise, but there were plenty of ships remaining. Prien nervously sent a torpedo into HMS *Royal Oak*. To his utter surprise there was no immediate reaction. The British sailors had assumed it was an internal explosion and quickly returned to their bunks. So Prien fired another three torpedos with devastating effect.

The crew of the *Oak* were even more confused as they went down, looking to the skies for signs of the Luftwaffe, still incredulous that it could possibly be a U-boat.

As 833 British sailors lost their lives trapped aboard the *Oak*, the *U-47* snuck away unnoticed through the southern channel, narrowly avoiding a British destroyer on the way out. And then it was back to Germany for beer and bratwurst with Hitler in Berlin.

This was one of the most daringly successful missions in the whole of the Second World War and gained Prien and his crew huge fame in Germany. Prien received the nickname Der Stier von Scapa Flow ('The Bull of Scapa Flow'); the emblem of a snorting bull was painted on the conning tower of *U-47*. Prien was awarded the Knight's Cross, the first sailor of the

U-boat service to receive this award. Even Winston Churchill grudgingly described Prien's feat as 'a remarkable exploit of professional skill and daring'.

However, the daredevil life of Prien did not last long. *U-47* was hit on her tenth patrol by one of her own circling torpedos in March 1941 and went down to a watery grave with 45 crewmen. Although he was at sea for less than two years, Prien's record stands high among the U-boat aces during the Second World War. He spent 238 days at sea, sinking 30 enemy vessels for a total tonnage of 193,808 GRT. William Shirer, the US journalist, wrote from Berlin on 18 October 1939:

> The place where the German U-boat sank the British battleship HMS *Royal Oak* was none other than the middle of Scapa Flow, Britain's greatest naval base. It sounds incredible. A world war submarine commander told me tonight that the Germans tried twice to get a U-boat into Scapa Flow during the last war, but both attempts failed and the submarines were lost.
>
> Captain Prien, commander of the submarine, came tripping into our afternoon press conference at the Propaganda Ministry this afternoon, followed by his crew – boys of eighteen, nineteen, twenty. Prien is thirty, clean-cut, cocky, a fanatical Nazi, and obviously capable. Introduced by Hitler's press chief, Dr Dietrich, who kept cursing the English and calling Churchill a liar, Prien told us little of how he did it. He said he had no trouble getting past the boom protecting the bay. British negligence must have been something terrific.

2001 Michel Desjoyeaux does it in 93 days in his 18-metre monohull *PRB* when he wins the Vendée Globe, the round-the-world solo yacht race.

2004 Francis Joyon takes 72 days in *IDEC*.

2004 Jean Luc van den Heede completes the fastest westward single-handed circumnavigation in *Adrien*, taking 122 days.

2005 Bruno Peyron takes 50 days in *Orange II*, a 38-metre catamaran with 13 crew.

2007–8 Francis Joyon completes the fastest single-handed voyage in 57 days in *IDEC II*.

Domination
2009 French come first, second and third in the Vendée Globe. Desjoyeaux wins again in *Foncia*, Armel Le Cleach is second in *Brit Air* and Marc Guillemot third, cementing the awesome reputation of French circumnavigators.

Top Ten Most Treacherous Waters

1. The Cretaceous Sea

The world's seas 80 million years ago are regarded as the most dangerous of all time due to the sheer number and ferocity of the marine predators, including the Giant Mosasaur, a voracious serpent up to 17 metres in length, with the appetite of a Great White Shark.

2. Cape Horn

The freezing waters round the cape of South America are particularly hazardous, owing to horrendous storms, a low coastal shelf and icebergs. It's possibly the greatest challenge in the world for sailing vessels and is littered with wrecks.

3. Gulf of Aden

Located in the Arabian Sea between Yemen and Somalia and nicknamed 'Pirate Alley', the Gulf is the most treacherous route on the globe today for any shipping that has to travel down the Suez Canal between the Mediterranean and the Indian Ocean. The lack of any stable government in Somalia has led to over 50 attacks and high ransoms demanded on captured yachts and tankers.

4. Straits of Messina

In Greek mythology two monsters guarded opposite sides of the Straits of Messina between Sicily and Calabria in Italy: Scylla was a six-headed creature that lived in a rock and regularly munched on sailors. Charybdis had a single gaping mouth that sucked in huge quantities of water and then belched it out three times a day, creating whirlpools. They were so close they posed an inescapable threat to passing sailors.

5. Baltic Sea

The waste from Swedish nuclear reactors, the Chernobyl accident in Russia and the currents from Sellafield in England make the Baltic the most radioactive in the world. In some areas the radioactivity is killing half the commercial fish stocks. There is only a 1 per cent exchange of water between the Baltic and the big oceans every year, so it is not a place to swim in a hurry.

6. Bermuda Triangle

This region of the North Atlantic between Bermuda, Puerto Rico and the southern tip of Florida has aquired almost mythical status due to the number of mysterious disappearances there. It is generally believed that around 20 aircraft and 50 other vessels have gone missing over the years. Increased electromagnetic waves can make compasses and other instruments fail, or when large deposits of methane clathrates (ice containing methane) on the sea floor melt they can release enough methane in the water to decrease the density and conceivably make a large ship suddenly sink without warning.

7. Southern Ocean

The ocean surrounding Antarctica is not for the faint-hearted. Apart from the ice-cold atmosphere, the Antarctic Circle also has the strongest average winds found anywhere on Earth. Cyclonic storms can be intense because of the temperature contrast between ice and ocean.

8. Mouth of the Columbia River

The bar where the river's mighty current collides with Pacific Ocean swells in Oregon, North America, is one of the most treacherous harbour entrances on the planet. Winter storms whip the sea into a ship-hungry maelstrom and it has earned the nickname 'Graveyard of the Pacific'.

9. Bay of Biscay

Between the western coast of France and northern Spain large parts of the continental shelf extend far into the bay, causing the shallow waters and rough seas for which the region is known. Some of the Atlantic's fiercest storms occur in the bay, especially during the winter months and many lives have been lost there.

10. The Scandinavian Seas

The realm of the Kraken, a giant, terrifying, many-armed mythological sea monster that could reach as high as a ship. Krakens would attack a vessel, wrap their arms around the hull and capsize it. The crew would drown or be eaten by the monster. With roots in Norse mythology, there were sightings of the Kraken in Norwegian waters in the fourteenth century and the Kraken could well have been based on sailors' observations of the giant squid we know today.

Lost to the Depths

> The depth is the only place to go and touch, feel and live the power of the ocean, but to reach it, it has to be done in harmony with it. When you dive with the sled you don't need your body, you have to be so relaxed that, at one point you just forget that you have one and that is when you meet the other person who lives inside you, the one in control of everything: your mind.

These are the words of Audrey Mestre, when she was interviewed in 2001. This beautiful Frenchwoman must have been born an amphibian. She grew up leaping into the water at every given opportunity – swimming and scuba-diving before she became a marine biologist. But it was free diving that became her greatest passion and led to her spiritual awakening in the magnificent depths of the deep blue.

In 1996 Mestre met her soulmate, the Cuban world free-diving champion Francisco 'Pipin' Ferreras, with whom she shared a complex romance bonded by a shared obsession with the ocean. They soon became free diving's golden couple, creating a seemingly untouchable bubble where they tested the limits of their minds and bodies by descending to unthinkable depths.

Mestre moved to Miami to be with Ferreras and in 2000, soon after they married, Mestre broke the female world record by free diving to a depth of 125 metres on a single breath of air at Fort Lauderdale. A year later she broke her own record, by descending to 130 metres.

Then, on 12 October 2002, in a dive off the coast of the Dominican Republic, Mestre attempted to break the world record of 171 metres. Clinging to a metal sled, she was carried down to the record depth after 1 minute 42 seconds, the deepest any human had ever dived on a single breath of air. This was a hybrid-aqua woman in action, a real mermaid with flowing chestnut tresses. But these are depths where a tin of beans would implode due to water compression. Her lungs would have been compressed to the size of small apples and her heart rate would have been as low as 20 beats per minute.

Disaster struck: a problem developed with the air-lift balloon as she started her ascent. Halfway up she fell unconscious – her three-minute dive had turned into an eight-and-a-half minute nightmare. By the time her husband could bring her unconscious body to the surface she was foaming at the mouth and it was too late. She was pronounced dead at a hospital on shore. She was only 28 years old.

Her death sent shock waves through the free-diving world and some experts alleged that Ferreras pushed her too far and too fast leading up to the dive that took her life.

But this was a sport finding its limits, a beautiful sport awash with accidents that also killed Frenchmen Loic Leferme and Cyril Isoardi, and caused blackouts and strokes in others. As Leferme himself said, 'You can't ban "no limits". It would be like trying to forbid people from climbing Everest. It's impossible.'

3 | Aviation

Burmese Balloonist

Burmese U Kyaw Yin (1873–1939) came to ballooning so late you could almost call him the flying pensioner. From the age of 60 he flew 55 times, though the British never granted him a licence to balloon abroad because he had taught himself.

In his childhood Kyaw Yin took to acrobatics, gymnastics, running and jumping, and learned from his parents and experienced elders some basic principles of balloon-making. He made a white cotton balloon which, when filled with hot air and smoke, could rise over three kilometres into the air with Kyaw Yin suspended precariously below on an iron bar.

When he first went up with his balloon he performed gymnastic acts on the iron bar as the balloon rose into the sky. He wore no protective clothing, just traditional Myanmar dress, and in 1930, on an island in the Kandaw Gyi Lake, Yangon, the balloon struck trees and Kyaw Yin dropped heavily onto a road used by cars. Luckily he only bruised his chin and legs. But it was a death-defying stunt every time he went up, much to the delight of the balloon-obsessed Burmese people, who otherwise largely preferred to send their fire balloons into the sky without anyone attached underneath.

British Civil Servant Maurice Collis wrote in his book *Into Hidden Burma*:

One day a man called Maung Kyaw Yin came to my house and asked permission to make a balloon ascent. The balloon, I learnt, was lifted by hot air, like the paper balloons sent up at festivals [...] Kyaw Yin, after prostrating himself to the four quarters of the sky [...] took hold of his trapeze, told his men to let go the rope so that he was whirled upwards, hanging head downwards from his bar. There was no wind and he went up straight, but after 250 feet the air in his balloon cooled and he began to descend. A slight draught now carried it over the sea. There was a shout from the crowd and a rush for the bank. But I had ordered the port launch, the *Jalinga*, to follow him in such a contingency, and as he was precipitated into the sea, the launch crew rescued him. The balloon lay on the sea, smoking like a dying dragon. Soon Kyaw Yin was seen arriving, standing on the roof of the *Jalinga*. The crowd gave him a great ovation. People were mad with joy. It was a great spectacle for quiet Mergui. Kyaw Yin pressed through the crowd to where I sat in my car. I gave him my hand.

His last balloon ascent was in Dawei in 1939, and he died later that year.

Sportsman of the Air

Few have ever had as much passion for aviation as the playboy Brazilian Alberto Santos-Dumont (1873–1932) – he dedicated himself to the conquest of the air at the turn of the twentieth century. The diminutive South American is still considered by many to be the father of aviation as he made the first ever public flight of an airplane, *L'Oiseau de Proie* (the Bird of Prey), on 23 October 1906. It was the first fixed-wing aircraft officially witnessed to take off, fly and land, though the Wright brothers were also making successful flights in private.

Son of a prosperous coffee-owning family, his passion was ignited for flight while he was studying in Paris. Santos-Dumont started flying when he hired and took lessons from an experienced balloon pilot. He quickly moved on to piloting balloons himself, and then designing his own balloons. In 1898, Santos-Dumont flew his first balloon design, the *Brasil*.

He soon turned to the design of steerable balloons (dirigibles or early airships) that could be propelled through the air in a particular direction rather than drift along with the breeze. Between 1898 and 1905 he built and flew 11 different airships, and with no air-traffic control to monitor him, he would glide along Paris boulevards at rooftop level and land where he fancied, whether it be to salute the president of France or cause a stir at a children's party. Usually he would land near the café of his choice for a long lunch.

To win the prestigious Deutsch de la Meurthe race (a competition to fly from Parc Saint Cloud to the Eiffel Tower and back in under 30 minutes), Santos-Dumont pulled out the stops to build dirigible number five. But this lost too much hydrogen gas and exploded, leaving him dangling in the basket from the side of the Trocadero hotel. With the help of the crowd he climbed to safety. As he had described himself, he was a true 'sportsman of the air'.

However, on 19 October 1901, after several attempts and trials, Santos-Dumont succeeded. Using dirigible number six, he made it back seconds before the cut-off. A last-minute rule change meant several days of vacillating by the committee of officials, but then Santos-Dumont was awarded the 100,000 francs prize money, of which he gave half to the poor of Paris and half to his workmen. His feats and generosity made him a celebrity around the world. The public and the press followed his exploits and Parisians affectionately dubbed him 'le petit Santos'. His final design was a monoplane called *Demoiselle*, the blueprint for which he handed over for free, failing to see the commercial potential from his altruistic perspective of the skies. He remains a great hero in Brazil and in the world of aviation.

The Perfect Landing

If there's ever a definition of a cool cat in crisis then it must Captain Chelsey Sullenberger, the American pilot whose life seem destined to be in the cockpit of the ill-fated US Airways Flight 1549 whose engines failed when he flew through a rogue flock of geese.

This is the man who is also a flight safety instructor and, as such, had the perfect preparation for the five-minute pressure crucible on board the crowded passenger plane that had just taken off from New York's La Guardia airport on 15 January 2009. Reacting with no more emotional intonation than if he were telling the 150 passengers the weather was fine and they had run out of Waldorf salad, he calmly uttered over the plane speaker the terrifying instruction, 'Brace for impact', before putting the plane down on the Hudson river as if it were a feathered glider.

Although his eerily silent plane was gliding lower and lower with no way of reaching a runway, Sullenberger could be heard talking to New York air-traffic controllers in what a senior investigator later called a 'very calm, collected exercise'. He alerted air-traffic control that the plane, code-named Cactus 1549, 'hit birds, lost thrust in both engines. We're turning back toward La Guardia.'

The air-traffic controller quickly made the arrangement and said, 'Try to land on runway three.'

'We're unable. We may end up in the Hudson,' Sullenberger coolly answered.

The air-traffic controller did not take this in.

'Unable,' Sullenberger calmly reiterated. Then, 'Not sure if we can make any runway – oh, what's over to our right? Anything in New Jersey, maybe Teterboro?'

Air-traffic control: 'You can land runway one at Teterboro.'

Sullenberger replied simply, 'We can't do it.'

'OK. Which runway would you like at Teterboro?' asked the audibly stressed air-traffic controller.

'We're gonna be in the Hudson,' Sullenberger conceded.

The air-traffic controller's request 'Say again, Cactus' was never answered.

Seconds later the controller announced the flight was off the radar, and the pilot of another plane came frantically on air with an incredulous voice, saying: 'I don't know, I think he said he was going in the Hudson.'

At that moment, Sullenberger brought the plane down on the river opposite midtown Manhattan, saving the lives of all 155

people on board. The only lives lost were those of the geese, which, federal safety officials confirmed, were in both engines.

Even when the plane had landed, Sullenberger made sure all the passengers were plucked to safety from the rafts, one by one, before he got off. When the moment arose, Sullenberger behaved with selfless and flawless bravery.

One assumes no one other than Clint Eastwood will be offered the role of the 57-year-old pilot when the inevitable Hollywood movie goes into production. It was no surprise when Sullenberger fielded congratulatory calls from former President George W Bush and President Barack Obama or when, within 24 hours of the landing, someone offered $10,000 to build his statue.

Sullenberger is the definitive flying machine. Originally from Texas but now living in California, he built model aeroplanes meticulously as a boy and even made headlines in the local paper for flying a crop duster at age 15. He served in the US Air Force from 1973 to 1980 and flew F-4 Phantom II fighter planes. He became a commercial pilot in 1980 for an airline later bought by US Airways and even more reassuringly Sullenberger started a California consulting firm, Safety Reliability Methods, two years ago to help apply the latest safety advances. One assumes it is not doing too badly now. It seems providence could not have picked a better man to land a passenger jet on a river.

Ten Fantastic Flying Machines Through Time

1. Rocket Chair
If the depictions of the Emperor Wan-Ha are to be believed, the ancient Chinese certainly considered the possibility of a rocket chair that could take off, though it's unlikely they ever made one.

2. Helical Air Screw
This was a much-vaunted spiral design in 1490 that the great Italian artist Leonardo da Vinci made to show how man could fly. He realised the screw-shaped device would rise if turned very quickly. The technology did not exist to try it out, but many experts say the modern-day helicopter was inspired by Leonardo.

3. Taffeta Wings
Besnier, a locksmith from Sable, France, managed to sustain himself in flight over a wide river in 1678, using hinged wings made of taffeta stretched over frames which he would flap alternately, using both arms and legs.

Flying Angels

Lily Litvak

There have been few more hardcore female fighter pilots than the Russian Lily Litvak. Stunningly beautiful with blonde hair and piercing grey eyes that coolly lined up 12 Luftwaffe planes before she shot them down, Lily was the matinee idol of the skies and known as the White Rose of Stalingrad. With these 12 kills to her credit, she was the Soviet Union's top female ace fighter pilot.

Russian women were not easily accepted into the military and her male comrades were not keen to let her fly until they saw the way she could dogfight. However, they were probably behind a practical joke that terrified Lily's female winger, Olga Yemshokova. When on a patrol at 3,657 metres, she spied a mouse twitching its nose at her in the cockpit.

'I know it sounds crazy – a fighter pilot frightened by a mouse – but I'd always had this fear of mice,' Olga said. 'And particularly now it was sitting on my lap looking up at me, in that tiny cockpit.' She admitted she 'could feel her flesh creeping' and a tingle down her spine as she opened the cockpit and flung the poor little mouse into the slipstream.

But Lily showed what women could achieve in the air. In September 1942, flying a Yak-1 with white roses painted on both sides of her cockpit, Lily shot down a Junkers Ju-88 and a Messerschmitt Bf-109 on only her second combat flight.

Lily then out-flew and out-fought German pilots to become an immediate Soviet hero, as well garnering male attention from all over the motherland, particularly from men whose eyes had popped out when they had flown with her. But Lily had already fallen in love with Lieutenant Alexi Salomaten, with whom she had flown in her first combat mission.

'Lily said it was agony up there sometimes when Alexi was being attacked. But of course it gave each of them an incentive to fight really well,' her mechanic, Ina Pasportnikova, recalled. 'Far from their love for each other affecting their concentration, I think it helped. Lily had always shown the sort of aggression you need to be a good fighter pilot. But her love for Alexi was the thing that turned her into a killer.'

Lily then survived an encounter with German cannon fire that left her with a limp. Soon afterwards, Alexi died in a crash. It all sharpened her killer instinct, which hardened into an obsession to bring down Germans. Her tenth victim, a German ace himself, survived to be confronted by her, and the Luftwaffe hero initially refused to believe he had been out-fought by a woman. Then the White Rose coldly explained the very manoeuvres that had outwitted him. 'The German's whole attitude, even his physical appearance, changed,' reported an eyewitness. 'He was forced to concede in the end that no one except the pilot who had beaten him could possibly have known, move by move, exactly how the fight had gone. There was no question of saluting the victor. He could not meet her eye. To have been shot down by a woman was more than he could bear.'

The day of her final mission, Lily had already flown four previous sorties. She was escorting a flight of Soviet bombers when her Yak was jumped by a flight of eight Bf-109s. On 1 August 1943, she was shot down during combat and went missing. She was 21 years old.

On 6 May 1990, USSR President Mikhail Gorbachev posthumously made her a Hero of the Soviet Union. A play about her, *White Rose*, was performed once in Coventry.

4. Silk Bag Balloon

The sons of a paper-bag manufacturer at Annonay, France, Joseph and Jacques Montgolfier used to play with inverted paper bags over an open fire, and fabricated a silk bag which, on 5 June 1783, they tried in the first ever public demonstration of a balloon. Five months later, physician Jean-François Pilâtre de Rozier and an audacious army officer, François Laurent d'Arlandes, flew nine kilometres at around 910 metres above Paris in the Montgolfiers' balloon. This was the first successful manned flight.

5. *Silver Dart*

By 1891 Briton Alexander Bell, who invented the telephone, had moved on to kites as the most stable structures for human flight, using a V-8 engine, a propeller and two wings made from bamboo and silk. On 23 February 1909, on the ice of Baddeck Bay in Canada, the *Silver Dart*, piloted by Canadian Douglas McCurdy, rose nine metres into the air and flew for a kilometre.

6. Graf Zeppelin

Zeppelins, a kind of rigid-balloon airship, were the brainchild of German Count Ferdinand Graf von Zeppelin, and technologically culminated in the *Graf Zeppelin* in the 1930s, an airship more than three times the length of a Boeing 747, which had a cruising speed of 110 kilometres per hour, and made regular flights from Europe to South America in which two dozen passengers had their own suites and dined at banquets.

7. Spitfire

This Second World War British fighter plane was the key mainstay of Fighter Command in its victory over the Luftwaffe in the Battle of Britain. Designed by Reginald Mitchell and feared by the Luftwaffe's pilots, the Spitfire had speed, firepower and incredible manoeuvrability. When asked by head of the Luftwaffe Hermann Goering what he needed to win the Battle of Britain, the Luftwaffe fighting ace, Adolf Galland, is said to have replied, 'A squadron of Spitfires.'

Hanna Reitsch

Reitsch would undoubtedly be recognised as the best woman pilot of the century if she had not been such a fanatical Nazi. She was the perfect advert for the Third Reich: young, daring, photogenic and blindly committed to the cause. There is no doubting her foolhardy bravery.

Reitsch left medical school to pursue her passion for flying, and was one of the first few people to cross the Alps in a glider.

As the world's first female test and helicopter pilot, Hanna flew everything the Third Reich had: from the first helicopter (the Focke-Achgelis) to the prototype of a piloted V-1 Flying Bomb. This took incredible courage. It was her suggestion that Adolf Hitler should create a suicide squadron of glider pilots. To this even Hitler was sceptical, believing it was not a good use of Germany's limited resources. But Reitsch persuaded him to adapt the pilotless V-1 into a kamikaze vehicle. She formed a suicide group, and was herself the first person to take the pledge: 'I hereby ... apply to be enrolled in the suicide group as a pilot of a human glider-bomb. I fully understand that employment in this capacity will entail my own death.'

Although she never got sent on the suicide mission she desired, she piloted a V-1 rocket in sub-orbital flight in the early 1940s (20 years before the first spaceman) and managed to land it at the astonishing speed of around 200 kilometres per hour. She was the only woman ever to be awarded the Iron Cross and Luftwaffe Diamond Clasp. She went on to set more than 40 altitude and endurance records in her lifetime, including the Women's World Record for distance and the Women's World Altitude record for gliders.

In 1945 Reitsch flew into a burning Berlin and landed beside a street full of Russian tanks on an improvised airstrip in the

Tiergarten near the Brandenberg Gate. She was by the side of her Führer when he shot himself in his bunker and she flew the last plane out of Berlin hours before the fall of the city. She was soon captured, and interrogated for 18 months after the war. Her father killed her mother, her sister and her sister's children, before killing himself during the last days of the war in their hometown of Hirschberg.

Beryl Markham

An aviatrix, a seductress, a horse breeder and a writer, Beryl Markham led an extraordinary life of adventure ahead of her time as a wild woman enjoying herself in a man's world. She played men at their own game in the air and on the ground.

Born Beryl Clutterbuck on 26 October 1902, she grew up in Kenya to be beautiful, independent and eccentric, and became the first licensed female horse trainer there. In 1929 she had an affair with King George V's son, the married Duke of Gloucester, and was paid £15,000 to keep quite over the scandal. Now independently wealthy and mingling with the notoriously decadent Happy Valley set, she had an affair with the pilot and hunter Denys Finch Hatton, the love interest in Karen Blixen's *Out of Africa*, and narrowly avoided accompanying him on his fatal flight.

Learning at the controls with British pilot Tom Black, with whom she had the next long-term affair, she took up flying. She worked for some time as a bush pilot before she set her sights on grander adventures. Markham decided to take on the Atlantic crossing by flying non-stop from England to New York, a flight no pilot had yet made, and one which would also make her the first woman to fly solo across the Atlantic. Several women had died trying. On 4 September 1936, she took off from Abingdon, UK, and after a 20-hour flight her

8. Rocket Belt

When this kind of one-man rocket pack was developed by Bell Aerosystems as the Bell Rocket Belt in the late 1950s, it gave a whole a new meaning to having a rocket up your arse. These early models had a 20-second flying time using a hydrogen-peroxide fuel and the 800-horse-powered rockets could propel the wearer to speeds of up to 97 kilometres per hour and over 18 metres into the air. In the Bond film *Thunderball*, Bond actually uses this very rocket belt to return to his Aston Martin DB5. In 1984, a rocket belt was used in the opening ceremony for the Olympic Games in Los Angeles.

>>>

9. MiG-21

This devastating instrument of war is the most produced combat aircraft since the Second World War. It's a supersonic jet fighter plane designed and built by the Mikoyan-Gurevich Design Bureau in the former Soviet Union. Nicknamed 'balalaika', due to the aircraft's resemblance to the Russian stringed musical instrument, it has been sold and used in conflicts all round the world.

10. F-22 Raptor

The US Air Force claims this is the most outstanding fighter plane ever built. It's a fifth-generation fighter aircraft using stealth technology produced by Lockheed Martin Aeronautics. Intended to be the leading US advanced tactical fighter in the early part of the twenty-first century, the Raptor is very expensive, about $140 million per unit, and as yet has no official operational history.

Vega Gull, the *Messenger*, ran out of fuel and she was forced to crash-land on Cape Breton Island, Nova Scotia. Though she was well short of her destination in New York, she now held both Atlantic crossing records: the first woman to cross on her own and the first person to cross from Europe to the USA without stopping en-route.

She then had time to turn her hand to writing her memoir, *West with the Night*, which gained widespread critical acclaim even from the likes of Ernest Hemingway, though he was less impressed by her wayward life. He said: 'This girl, who is to my knowledge very unpleasant and we might even say a high-grade bitch, can write rings around all of us who consider ourselves as writers ... it really is a bloody wonderful book.'

She was celebrated as an aviation pioneer throughout her wild and chequered life and when she died in 1986 the International Astronomical Union named an impact crater on the planet Venus after her.

Flying Car: The First Ever Crossing of the Strait of Gibraltar

It is an unremarkable Thursday morning in Morocco on the Spanish military base at Ceuta, which sits amid tall modern apartment blocks and gas pylons not far from the old walled city. It is a little gusty as usual and the guards walking on the helistrip are smoking cigarettes and drinking hot chocolate.

Suddenly there is a pan-pan distress safety call on the radio from the Strait of Gibraltar. It is a very excited voice shrieking in the Queen's English. Twenty minutes later a spectre looms out of the sky like a giant whirring bug and starts to nose-dive towards the narrow isthmus. Dangling and swinging under a wing it comes in at 110 kilometres per hour and looks out of control. But just as it looks as though it will miss the strip altogether, the pilot violently cuts the throttle and slam-dunks the aircraft into the runway, head-butting and breaking the windscreen as it comes to halt.

It has just come over the high seas from Tarifa, across the Strait of Gibraltar, on surely one of the first landmark adventures of the twenty-first century. Because this is no ordinary flying machine.

It's a prototype flying car – and the first roadworthy one to take to the skies and make a perilous crossing. As the Spanish soldiers curiously approach, a wind-burned Englishman in a flying suit leaps from the car and starts jumping up and down like a schoolboy with a golden tuck voucher.

Since the first flying-car prototype in 1949, there has been a global quest to find the money and the magic formula to concoct a flying car people can buy: pioneering Canadian Paul Moller has spent millions developing his hybrid flying car over three decades; there have been ingenious contraptions in France; the Pentagon is putting money into a military scout-craft project; and there's a 'roadable' aircraft being tested in Boston by corporate giants Terrafugia Inc. But no one has been able to assemble a high-performance car that flies.

This experiment was firmly in the tradition of mad, magnificent men in their flying machines dabbling with the unknown. The car that has landed does not look like most people's idea of a flying car. It does not pay a wistful glance to

Chitty Chitty Bang Bang. It's a souped-up buggy flying beneath a giant canopy that sails above the car in flight. It's the latest in paramotor technology and the car is the heaviest object ever to be carried by this technology. In flight mode a fan motor drives it forward and the wing takes it up and up. It's an extraordinary achievement of design.

The maverick pilot is the gentleman adventurer Neil Laughton, an ex-Royal Marine and SAS soldier who, at 45, still has a rarefied nose for derring-do. The two-seater Skycar is the brainchild of 29-year-old Giles Cardozo, or 'the boy genius' as Laughton affectionately refers to his wing man and co-pilot later on the trip. Cardozo, the madcap engineer of the paramotor world, pieced together the Skycar in his Dorset barn.

On that crisp February morning in 2009 they were all set. The car was primed, the wind was an acceptable 48 kilometres per hour and the film crew making a documentary were ready to fly alongside in a chopper. Moreover, Laughton had used his connections in the forces to contact the Royal Navy, who had willingly positioned HMS *Sabre* in the Strait on rescue duty.

At 10 a.m. on Tarifa beach, Laughton raced down the sand, took off and swirled into the sky. He made it up to 15 metres but could not go higher as the trimming on the wing seemed to be wrong – it started to spin and go out of control. 'It was unflyable. I was swinging around like a monkey and I knew I was going to crash,' he said. 'I heaved my arse out of my seat as quickly as I could and crouched on the side ready to jump.'

Then all of a sudden his luck changed. A gust hit the wing and spun the car round and up in the direction of the shore. 'I realised I had a chance – I leaped back in the seat and controlled it into the shore and landed on the beach. I was relieved to be alive but I put my head in my hands.'

Cardozo ran up 'as white as a sheet' with the dream seemingly over. But they decided to trim the wing a couple of centimetres to speed up the ascent and an hour later they realised there was one last chance to make or break the expedition.

'My adrenalin was really pumping. I was frightened but very focused,' Laughton said. 'The take-off is always a real buttock clencher but I held my breath and I was away again.' This time the car rose up and ascended all the way to 305 metres. The height brings more safety because it buys more time if anything goes wrong to deploy the emergency canopy or correct the direction.

'I felt very relaxed up there, just below the cloudline, flying over ships and ferries, and I started cruising over without any problem. I had a moment of peaceful bliss above the sea.'

'It's incredible to fly, actually very simple. It's surreal when you first take off, suddenly being in a car in the air. I had to stop playing with the steering wheel when I went airborne, which is not changing the direction. It's controlled by cables and pedals linked to the wing.'

But the serene moment didn't last for long. 'I got a call on the radio, saying I couldn't land at the private landing site in Morocco due to a military exercise, so I made a pan-pan call to Ceuta.'

Then the GPS system stopped working. 'I had to navigate blind as I came in to the tip of Africa. I knew to head to the harbour where the ships were coming in, and then I was over buildings, a children's school and some gas pylons about nine metres below me and I could see the airstrip surrounded by water on three sides and buildings on the other. It was a very tough place to land.

'I nose-dived in, nearly misjudged it, but came in with an ungainly slam dunk, a crash landing really. The steering-column pin sheared off, the chassis bent, a rear tyre burst and I whacked my head into the windscreen and smashed it. But it was a huge relief and a real pleasure – I knew no one had done this before. It was a real first.'

He had travelled just over 19 kilometres at a speed of 56 knots on a 25-minute flight. He had been very lucky. As fellow expedition member Toby Kilner added: 'When he was coming in to land I was very scared. I only gave him a 20 per cent chance of survival if he hit the water. Neil's got balls the size of coconuts.'

Meanwhile Laughton's wife, Caroline, was preparing baby food for his children, Oscar and Scarlett, at their home in Sussex. She had a call to say he was going across and then another when he landed, saying: 'Darling, I've made it, but got to go, the military are after me.'

The Spanish soldiers, utterly bemused by what had happened, surrounded Laughton when he landed and took his passport. 'They released me quickly but then I spent eight hours at the border with Morocco and they sent me back to Spain on the ferry with the Skycar. It was very funny when the staff on the ferry realised I was the same guy who had flown over them earlier in the day.'

The Skycar could be very popular. An executive producer from the James Bond films appeared at Dunsford airfield in Surrey when they were practising flights to ask about the possibility of a Skycar appearing in one of the next 007 movies.

Influential Flying Myths

Daedalus and Icarus

In Greek myth Daedalus was an eccentric figure
associated with artifice, puzzle and creation.
He moved to Crete with his son Icarus to become
resident architect for the wealthy King Minos,
which culminated in him designing the
dreaded labyrinth for the Minotaur,
a half-man, half-bull monster
to which 14 Athenian youths
were sacrificed every year;
however, when young Theseus
arrived, Daedalus gave him the secret
to the labyrinth and Theseus slew the Minotaur,
as the famous myth goes.

But Deadalus was now in a pickle with King Minos
and had to flee. He had been carefully observing the
grace of eagles in flight and experimenting in his workshop
with eagle feathers knitted together with bees' wax to make
wings fit for humans. Now was the time to test them. He and
Icarus attached the wings to their bodies and jumped off the
cliffs of Crete, hoping to glide all the way to Sicily over the
Aegean Sea.

Daedalus gave firm fatherly instructions not to fly too close to
the sea to avoid dampening the feathers with water, nor too
high to the sun for fear the wax would melt. But Icarus was so
excited by the experience he forgot and flew too close to the
sun. The wax turned to liquid, the feathers came apart and
Icarus plunged to his death in the sea, close to an island that is
now called Ikaria.

Emperor Shun

This is the first ever parachuting story. Before 2000 BC legend has it that the Chinese emperor Shun escaped a burning tower by the use of two large reed hats. Such hats are still worn in areas of China today and can be over a metre wide. If Shun had been a lightweight man, the broad reed hat may well have acted as an effective parachute to get him to the ground safely.

Wayland the Smith

In Northern Europe, Wayland the Smith had a reputation a little like that of Daedalus. He was a legendary smith and craftsman who was captured by a Swedish king called Nidud and forced to work for him on an island. Wayland soon gained his revenge by secretly killing Nidud's two sons and making treasures for Nidud fashioned from their skulls and teeth. He then seduced their sister Bodvild and made his escape with a pair of mechanical wings he had forged in his island workshop.

Sluagh

In Celtic mythology the Sluagh were a troublesome group of winged evil spirits, haunting the living and searching for the souls of other sinners to capture. West-facing windows were sometimes kept closed to keep them out in Scotland and Ireland.

Smaj

In Serbian mythology, the Smaj are the main guardians of Serbia and take the form of winged male mortals who can shoot fire as they fly.

Kanae

In Polynesian mythology, Kanae is a semi-deity or spirit who can transform himself into a flying fish.

Balepa

In Lakalai mythology on New Britain Island, a balepa is a corpse wrapped in its funeral mat forever floating over its hometown.

Skydiving Record

As part of what can only be described as extreme aviation research, US Air Force Colonel Joe Kittinger agreed to take part in Project Excelsior. This entailed the experienced airman donning a pressurised suit and jumping from a hot-air balloon at very high altitudes with temperatures of around - 94 degrees. He lost consciousness in the first jump from 23,286 metres on 16 November 1959, and was saved by the automatic parachute. For his third jump, in 1960, he leaped from 31,333 metres (31 kilometres). He survived to tell of the four and a half minutes of freefall and the speeds of 988 kilometres per hour. He opened his chute at 5,486 metres to land as a world-record holder – the most death-defying skydive in history.

A Day in the Life of...

Female Puma pilot in the RAF with four operational tours in Iraq

❝ The morning started like any other day in Morocco. I was there serving with my helicopter squadron on exercise supporting the Army. I'd been there almost a month and had come to love flying over and drinking up the rich tapestry of the Moroccan countryside. Our task was to transport the soldiers from A to B while they conducted essential training prior to deploying on operations to less hospitable nations. Such was the nature of the tasking that we were also able to do some training of our own. I was a junior pilot at this stage so I was being trained on dust-landing techniques, mountain-flying techniques and was learning how to handle a helicopter while very heavy in a hot environment – much more demanding than in the UK climate. In a 'hot and high' environment such as the Atlas Mountains, the rotor blades produce significantly less lift, due to the low air density. Consequently, the engines have to work harder to keep the aircraft aloft and there is little power left in reserve, hence much less margin for error. Your control has to be smooth and considered, not aggressive or reactive. It had been a huge learning curve but I had loved every minute of it. My training complete, my final mission was to carry out a pairs low-level sortie.

We carefully briefed the route we were going to take through the mountains. Helicopters routinely fly at just over 15 metres (about tree-top height), although we can go lower for tactical training, so we have to keep our eyes peeled for obstructions, such as houses, trees and wires and fly around them. We also take care to avoid over-flying livestock. Initially my aircraft would be the No. 2 in the formation, so we would be following the lead aircraft at fairly close, but not unsafe, quarters. We conducted the first part of the sortie without mishap and then changed the lead after a quick suck of gas at a refuel site in the mountains. Having crossed over a ridge of high mountains we then settled into a low-level route that scoured the desert floor and followed the line of several wadis that had been cut into the earth by ancient rivers. The gorge then opened into a valley, in the bottom of which was a little mountain pass. Our route followed this winding road through the valley. It was a moment when all my mountain and valley flying techniques came to the fore as I manoeuvred the aircraft round the twists and turns of the mountain pass.

The other pilot in our crew was scanning

the map, warning me of the next turn and of any obstructions that were marked on the map. Not all obstructions were marked, however, as we were about to learn.

As I rounded a corner I observed some huts. I instinctively started to climb, aware that habitation is usually fed with electricity. And that means wires. I climbed up out the valley and we saw a set of high-tension power cables pass beneath us and then parallel our track on our right-hand side. The other pilot commented at this stage on how difficult they were to see. I glanced right and was slightly unnerved to see that the wires were invisible to the naked eye. The only things that made these cables perceptible were the pylons that connected them; tall monstrous structures standing around 60 metres high. These cables were now diverging from us to the right across the plateau. I was content that the wires were no longer a threat to us I was about to descend back into the valley when I heard the other pilot cry 'F**k' and deflect the controls back and left, initiating a climbing left-hand turn. He had seen a pylon above us on the left hand side of the valley. Totally unexpected. I had barely time to process this when I heard an almighty bang and the canopy shattered.

What followed took about 2 seconds, but seemed to last a lifetime, just like in all the films. I realized we had just impacted wires. I envisaged the aircraft with no rotor blades and assumed that it would shortly catapult into the ground. I recognized at this point that I was going to die in a helicopter accident. I felt neither sad, nor scared. Just accepting.

Then I heard the other pilot shout, 'Fly the aircraft, fly the aircraft!' and I realised that the aircraft, rather than somersaulting towards the ground, remarkably, was in straight and level flight. Life resumed its normal pace at that point and I immediately became aware of a loud rushing sound through a huge gap in what used to be the canopy. The section of canopy that remained was a fragmented mess, which made forward visibility a little tricky. The other pilot had automatically lowered the gear and I shouted something about the engine instruments looking normal – the Puma has two engines but after impacting wires some eight centimetres in diameter, the potential for an engine failing, or even both, became a frightening reality. In addition, the possibility of wires being wrapped around the gearbox (which attaches the rotor blades to the engines) and the potentially catastrophic implications of that, hung over all the crew with a deep sense of foreboding and it was agreed that we should get the aircraft on the ground as soon as possible. The other pilot then attempted to transmit a MAYDAY call along the lines of 'MAYDAY MAYDAY MAYDAY we've hit the f***ing wires', but the mountains blocked our transmissions. My crewman spotted a suitable field in the bottom of the valley which looked big enough to fit two helicopters in, and talked me round the corner into the field. Although we had briefed the wind direction before take-off,

MAYDAY MAYDAY MAYDAY we've hit the f***ing wires

this is usually of little help in the mountains due to local funnelling effects, so there followed a short discussion to ascertain the wind direction before we settled on our landing direction, which, luckily, turned out to be spot on. I was yelling my intentions to the crew all the time because of the noise, but other than that it was a normal approach. I flew the aircraft as smoothly as possible and made as few power demands on it as I could, concerned that any large control movements might exacerbate any damage, and kept an eagle eye on the engine instruments for slight changes or deteriorations. All pilots will tell you that it's drummed into you during training to always plan for the worst when flying.

This training was starting to kick in now. I knew that if one of the engines packed up on approach I would be committed to the field and would have to make the best of it. A Puma can fly on one engine if it has sufficient airspeed, but as you reduce your speed on approach there comes a point when the aircraft will simply sink if only one engine is operating. In fact this may even be the case when both engines are operating at high altitude, which we were. Of course flying the approach into wind will help your situation, but only so much. I have to admit, despite the pressing nature of our situation, I remember feeling quite exhilarated and keen to step up to the challenge. (Had we in fact lost an engine, the other pilot, 'Peebs', would have been more than equal to the task. During one of his operational tours in Iraq his Puma suffered an engine failure. Deep in hostile territory and in the black of night he managed to land the aircraft safely in an area no bigger than a tennis court.) In any event, the aircraft was a tough old bird and got us safely on the ground, despite being pretty beaten up. Luckily, nobody was badly hurt (though tiny shards of canopy had scratched my visor and I had a small cut on my cheek, which I thought made me look very heroic at the time).

On the ground I needed a cigarette and the loo very badly. Then I apologised to the local Moroccans for destroying what was surely the village's only power supply, and I found out that we were the fourth aircraft to come down in the area after hitting wires. I will never forget that day. The day we cheated death. 9

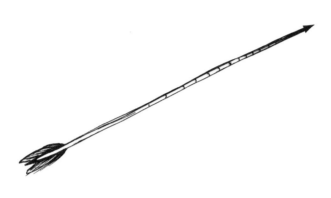

Samurai

The Tradition

It is difficult for anyone not to step back a little in awe of the traditions of the Japanese samurai, a class of military warriors whose codes were steeped in spirituality and self-sacrifice.

Samurai led their lives according to the ethics of *bushido*, 'the way of the warrior'. This combined the most intense respect for ancestry with a highly prized and unyielding code of conduct.

Every samurai aimed to become a heroic addition to his family, so that tales of his feats would be invoked by future generations. They sought immortality and glorious feats, the ultimate of which was death on the battlefield.

Brief History

794–1192   *Heian Period*

The samurai's influence began to grow when powerful landowners hired private warriors to protect their properties. Towards the end of the Heian period, two military clans, the Minamoto and the Taira, had grown so strong that they seized control over the country and fought against one another in a war for supremacy.

1192–1333   *Kamakura Period*

In 1185 the Minamoto were victorious and Minamoto Yoritomo set up a military government in Kamakura in 1192. As shogun, the highest military officer, he became the ruler of Japan.

Muromachi Period

During this, the Muromachi period, the chaotic 'Era of the Warring States', Japan consisted of dozens of independent states which constantly fought each other. Consequently, the demand for samurai was very high. Between the wars, many samurai worked on farms, where they were also able to train and to hone their combat skills.

Azuchi-Momoyama Period

When Toyotomi Hideyoshi united Japan in around 1591, he introduced a rigid social caste system which was later completed by his successors. Hideyoshi forced all samurai to decide between life on the farm and warrior life, which would require them to live in fortified towns under a feudal lord. Furthermore, he forbade anyone but the samurai to arm themselves with a sword.

Edo Period

During this era the samurai stood at the top of the social hierarchy, followed by farmers, artisans and merchants. All samurai were forced to live in castle towns and received income from their lords in the form of rice. Masterless samurai were called *ronin* and, like untamed rogue elephants, caused minor troubles during the early days of this period.

With the fall of Osaka Castle in 1615 relative peace prevailed in Japan for about 250 years. As a result, the importance of martial skills declined and most samurai became bureaucrats, teachers or artists. In 1868 Japan's feudal era came to an end, and the samurai class was abolished. But the spirit of *bushido* lived on, especially during the Second World War, when the code of conduct was evoked by the kamikaze pilots in the Japanese Air Force.

The Sixteenth Century:
A Golden Age for the Samurai

Clans

There were different levels of samurai: the elite would be the inner group of loyal and established men whose service to a clan would go back generations; another level would include those closely bound by marriage and those who had a link to a clan from bygone feats on the battlefield; yet another level would include those who had risen through the ranks, benefiting from their military prowess and dedication.

But there were other complex structures involved; sometimes an *ikki* was formed by those who had no clan or similar powerbase to belong to. Such allegiances were broadly democratic but they were looked upon as a lower social class, regardless of the fact that they were often a combative match for the clan-based samurai. Eventually the *ikki* lost their strength when the rural classes were disarmed.

Life and Training

A samurai's life was based around the castle and estates of his clan. The closest family retainers would live in the keep with their lord, but those lower down the hierarchy would live in complexes or stockades nearby.

A samurai would wake at sunrise. Much of his time would be spent mastering sword and fighting techniques (exercises that became the foundation for modern martial arts). *Suburi* was a technique similar to shadow boxing and *kata* was a type of practice in which all moves were prescribed in advance to avoid danger.

To avoid accidentally killing each other, they often used dummy weapons, such as a *tampo yuri* (a practice spear with a padded end) and a *bokuto*, which was a wooden sword weighing exactly the same as the real thing. With these weapons they could enjoy inflicting severe bruises on one another and causing the odd broken bone. Such injuries livened up the training sessions and helped to toughen them up.

They often practised *tsumeru*, which involved a victory on points. Decisive blows were made but not followed through, meaning that real swords could be used if the samurai were agile enough. The skill was brought to perfection by Miyamoto Musashi, who could so perfectly control his sword that he could sever a grain of rice on another man's forehead without spilling a drop of blood.

One way the samurai could practise for real was by executing criminals – most would have lopped off a head by the time they were 15. From the age of five they were also allowed to use real swords, but only to practise on dogs.

Leisure

Most samurai were educated and so time away from martial activities was spent painting, reading, writing and recounting epic war tales, which gave them inspiration in their own lives. They would play Japanese chess and a strategic game with black and white stones called *igo*. They also enjoyed the tea ceremony and, when not drinking from fine porcelain cups, played their own version of football or hacky sack called *kemari*, which involved keeping a ball in the air and passing to each other.

Other training techniques

Iai: the emphasis was on on drawing the sword and striking a deadly blow in one rapid movement.

Yabusam: archery performed on horseback. The samurai would gallop past small wooden targets, firing arrows.

Daky: similar to an early form of polo, though it was more like lacrosse on horseback. It involved two teams of five riders each trying to score at the same goal while carrying nets attached to long poles.

Food and Drink

A samurai lived a frugal life with a diet consisting of rice, vegetables, soya, fish, seaweed, salt and fruit, often accompanied by pickled plums and pickled ginger. Delicacies included bears' paws, badger and crackling from wild boar. They drank tea and for something stronger they had the lethal spirit *sake*.

Appearance

The samurai tried to set an example by their appearance and by any medieval standards they were squeaky clean. It was crucial for their self-discipline. They would cut their fingernails and toenails and often be clean-shaven. Their hair would be pulled back in a neat ponytail except in battle when it was let down and tied with a headband. And their armour was glorious.

Crucial Weapons

The *katana* is the weapon synonymous with the samurai. It is regarded as the soul of the warrior and the tool integral to the samurai's skill as a warrior. Together with a small dagger known as a *wakizashi*, the pair of weapons were called a *daisho* (meaning 'big and small'), which was the basis of the samurai weaponry throughout their existence. It was also their badge.

They believed the *katana* was so precious that they often gave them names and considered them to be living things. It served as both sword and shield as the curved blade, which was over 60 centimetres long, was perfect for deflecting blows as well as inflicting them. After a male bushi (another word for samurai) child was born, he would receive his first sword in a ceremony called *mamori-gatana*. The sword was merely a charm worn by boys under five but, upon reaching the age of 13, in a ceremony called *genpuku*, they would be given a real sword and armour and become a samurai.

The *wakizashi* daggar was a samurai's honour blade and never left his side. He would sleep with it under his pillow and it would be taken with him when he entered a house, even if he had to leave his main weapons outside. The *wakizashi* was used to commit the ritualised suicide of *seppuku*.

The *yumi* was a bamboo longbow often used from horseback. It had a range of about 50 metres. In the fifteenth century, the *yari*, which was a spear, also became a popular weapon; it was particularly useful for skewering foot soldiers from horseback. The *kusari-gama* was a sickle and chain.

The later half of the sixteenth century saw the introduction of the arquebus, enabling some warlords to raise effective armies from masses of peasants. But muzzle-loading firearms were not embraced by the samurai. The fact that anyone could get their hands on one and shoot down a noble warrior was a dishonourable affront to the samurai tradition.

Shudo and Bido

This was the name for the traditional love bonds between a seasoned samurai and a novice, reckoned to be 'the flower of the samurai spirit' or 'the beautiful way'. It formed the real basis of the samurai aesthetic. It was crucial to their ethos and one of the main ways in which their skills and traditions were passed down from one generation to another. The devotion that two samurai would have for each other would be almost as great as that which they had for their clan lord.

More samurai terminology

Katana sword

Yumitori a bowman

Kurusu skill of archery

Daimyo clan

Ronin a samurai with no attachment to a clan

Koku 180 litres of rice, enough to feed a man for a year and the method of payment

Uruwashii a cultured warrior

Buke a martial house or a member of such a house

Mononofu an ancient term meaning a 'warrior'

Shi a word roughly meaning 'gentleman'

Tsuwamono an old term for a soldier

Marriage

A samurai was too busy for elaborate courtship; thus, marriage was arranged by someone with the same or higher rank. While for those samurai in the upper ranks this was a necessity, it was a formality for those in the lower classes, who were permitted to marry commoners. A samurai could have a mistress but her background was strictly checked. In many cases, this relationship was treated like a marriage. If the woman were a commoner, a messenger would be sent with betrothal money or a note for exemption of tax to ask for her parents' acceptance, which was often readily granted. Divorce was possible in extenuating circumstances, say, if there were no male heir; however, adoption could be arranged. A samurai could divorce for personal reasons, even if he simply did not like his wife, but this was generally avoided as it would cause embarrassment to the samurai who had arranged the marriage. A samurai's wife would be dishonoured and allowed to commit *jigai* (female *seppuku*) if she were cast off.

Philosophy

Buddhism, Zen and Confucianism influenced the samurai culture. Zen meditation provided an important resource to help calm and clear the mind. The Buddhist concept of reincarnation and rebirth led some samurai to abandon torture and needless killing, while others even gave up violence altogether and became Buddhist monks. The most defining role that Confucianism played was to stress the importance of the lord–retainer relationship.

War and Combat

The night before battle a samurai would try to clear his mind and abstain from sex and venison, a meat thought to be too stimulating. The glory of being the first into battle and the first to die was a sought-after honour, but it sometimes upset the ordered plans of the military general. Gathering as many bloody enemy heads as possible was a strong tradition and all were resolved to die with their corpses facing the right way (i.e. not in retreat).

Japanese armour was effective. It took more than one stroke to kill a man unless a helmet was spliced in two by a strong blow from a sword. Samurai tended to single out an enemy to engage in man-to-man combat, and those with high-quality armour would be prime targets for glory seekers.

Minor cuts were treated with a coagulant called *yomogi* (mugwort) and wounded intestines would be covered with dried horse faeces, but samurai often bled to death from their wounds. They would fight to the death and sometimes a little after. The theory was that even after your head was cut off you could still manage one last stroke. Only a still corpse was no longer a danger. Survivors of the vanquished would simply be absorbed in the ranks of the victors with minimum fuss, if they hadn't managed to commit suicide first ...

Death

A well-documented feature of *bushido* was that a samurai should be prepared to kill himself. In the seventeenth century, a study of the samurai known as the *hagakure* emphasised the need to give one's life at any moment:

> One should expect death daily, so that, when the time comes, one can die in peace. Calamity, when it occurs, is not so dreadful as was feared. It is foolish to torment oneself beforehand with vain imaginings. Tranquillise your mind every morning, and imagine the torment when

you may be torn and mangled by arrows, guns, lances and swords, swept away by great waves, thrown into fire, struck down by thunderbolts, shaken by earthquakes, falling from a precipice, dying of disease or dead from an unexpected accident: die every morning in your mind, and then you will not fear death. Once that has been achieved – when one attains a mind of 'no-mindness' – then one can execute extraordinary deeds. In bushido honour comes first. Therefore, every morning and evening, have the idea of death vividly impressed in your mind.

The first tradition of suicide involved agreeing to be buried alive with the clan leader when he died, though this quickly became replaced in popularity by *seppuku* (disembowelment) or *harakiri* (belly-slitting), which led to a more aesthetically pleasing show of valour from the samurai. Moreover, the guts were regarded as the body's spiritual centre and soul.

One should expect death daily

Harakiri involved sitting cross-legged, taking a *wakizashi* or a *tanto* (small dagger) and skewering it into the left side of the abdomen, ripping it across the lower stomach and giving it a final twist upwards toward the chest. This would precipitate the intestines falling out, whereupon many samurai would pull them out further and spread them out as a gruesome act of bravado. As disembowelment involved a long and painful death the samurai would proffer his neck for decapitation. The ideal stroke would ideally leave enough skin and muscle to prevent the head rolling away. It was a symbol of the will and courage of the samurai to die in such excruciating fashion – it showed that he could rise above other men in honour and death.

Warriors

Torii Mototada 1539–1600

Mototada was a feudal lord in the service of Tokugawa Ieyasu who volunteered to remain behind and look after Fushimi Castle on the eve of the battle of Sekigahara. Though the fortification was indefensible, he made the commitment out of loyalty and pledged that he and his men would fight to the finish and not be taken alive. In a ferocious stand, Torii's garrison of 2,000 men held out for ten days against Ishida Mitsunari's 40,000 warriors.

Torii wrote to his son Tadamasa:

> It is not the Way of the Warrior to be shamed and avoid death even under circumstances that are not particularly important. It goes without saying that to sacrifice one's life for the sake of his master is an unchanging principle. That I should be able to go ahead of all the other warriors of this country and lay down my life for the sake of my master's benevolence is an honour to my family and has been my most fervent desire for many years.

Both father and son cried when they parted because they knew they would never see each other again. Torii's father and grandfather had served the Tokugawa family before him and his own brother had already been killed in battle. Torii's actions shaped history as Tokugawa had time to successfully raise an army and win at Sekigahara.

Miyamoto Musashi 1584–1645

Musashi was one of the greatest swordsmen that has ever lived. There was little he could not do with a sabre in his hand, earning the rank of *kensei* (sword-saint). He was born in the

village of Miyamoto in 1584, a descendant of the Fujiwara clan. He was only 13 when he first dallied with single combat, challenging the swordsman Arima Kihei. Although Musashi was very young he defeated the samurai, striking him repeatedly with a stick so violently that Kihei died.

Musashi learned to wield a *katana* in one hand, instead of the usual two-handed grip, and began to develop a style of fighting using two swords. At 16 he left home to begin his *musha-shugyo*, a pilgrimage on which a warrior would become a *ronin* and establish a reputation from the duels he fought while travelling. Musashi lived like a scruffy vagabond – he never cut his hair, never married and never even bathed. He became the archetypal unkempt, invincible bachelor. When he was 21 he fought Yoshioka Seijuro, head of a family in Kyoto, armed only with a *bokken* (a heavy wooden practice sword). Musashi defeated Seijuro, leaving him gravely wounded. He recovered but hung up his swords and cut off his samurai topknot in shame.

Musashi's *musha-shugyo* made him a famous in his own lifetime. He defeated swordsman after swordsman, and many warriors armed with other weapons. He fought and killed Shishido Baiken, a noted master of *kusari-gama*, by distracting him with a thrown dagger and he used a slender wooden wand to defeat the master swordsman Muso Gonnosuke.

In 1612, Musashi thrashed the noted master swordsman Sasaki Kojiro in one of his most famous duels. It is said that he arrived late, and that he fought armed with a *bokken* he had carved from an oar on his way to the duel, while Kojiro used a real sword. He mocked Kojiro when the older man threw aside his scabbard, remarking that he would not need it again. The two men struck hard at each other's heads, and while Kojiro's blade cut through Musashi's headband, Musashi struck faster, and the impromptu *bokken* split Kojiro's skull before he could complete his blow.

Another account has him defeating a swordsman simply by guarding himself with a *tessen* (an iron defensive fan) until his opponent became tired and submitted.

In his later life, Mushashi was a more humble man. By the age of 30, he had fought and won over 60 duels. Musashi eventually retired to a cave where he completed the famous *Book of Five Rings* (a treatise on martial arts) a few weeks before his death.

Tomoe Gozen

1157–1247

One of the rare examples of a female samurai, Gozen was a fearless warrior during the Gempei War. Some sources say she was the attendant or wife of Yoshinaka and fought as one of his captains against Yonitomo's forces at the battle of Awazu in 1184, when she took down at least one enemy; however, Yoshinaka was defeated. Reports of her fate remain conflicted: either she fled the battlefield and became a nun or she stayed and died with her leader. An extract from the *Tale of Heike* sums up her story better:

> Tomoe was especially beautiful, with white skin, long hair and charming features. She was a remarkably strong archer, and as a swordsman she was a warrior worth a thousand, ready to confront a demon or a god, mounted or on foot. Whenever a battle was eminent, Yoshinake sent her out as his first captain, equipped with strong armour, an oversized sword, and a mighty bow, and she performed more deeds of valour than any other of his warriors.

Foreign Samurai

1564–1620 *William Adams*

The English sailor William Adams (1564–1620) was the first Caucasian to become a samurai. After his ship was wrecked he was washed up on the shores of Japan. The Shogun Tokugawa Ieyasu took an immediate liking to Adams and appointed him as his senior diplomatic and trade adviser on all matters related to Western powers and civilization and, after he had learned Japanese, he was presented with two swords representing the authority of a samurai.

It was decreed that William Adams the sailor was dead and that Miura Anjin, a samurai, was born. He was granted a fief in Hemi with eighty or ninety husbandmen. He wrote 'God hath provided for me after my great misery' meaning his fortunes had lifted from shipwrecked to samurai.

1556–1623 *Jan Joosten van Lodenstein*

The one and only Dutch samurai, van Lodenstein was a colleague of Adams's, and was given similar privileges by Tokugawa Ieyasu after he was selected to be a confidant on European politics and affairs. It appears Joosten also became a samurai, and was given the name of Yayosu and a residence within Ieyasu's castle at Edo. Joosten was allowed to take a Japanese wife and was given a permit to engage in foreign trade, though he drowned at sea in 1623.

1838–1911 *Jules Brunet*

The Frenchman was a member of the first French military mission to Japan in 1867 to train the army of Shogun Tokugawa Yoshinobu. Brunet took a very active role during the Boshin War between partisans of the Shogun, with whom

Brunet sided, and partisans of the restoration of Emperor Meiji. They formed a Franco-Japanese leadership, with Otori Keisuke as commander-in-chief and Jules Brunet as second-in-command. The final stand occurred in the city of Hakodate, where in June 1869 the shogunate forces, only numbering 800 samurai, lost a close-fought battle to the 8,000-strong Imperial Army. Brunet survived and retuned to France. The Hollywood film *The Last Samurai*, starring Tom Cruise, was largely based on his exploits.

Edward Schnell

The Prussian served the Aizu domain as a military instructor and procurer of weapons from 1868–9. He was granted the Japanese name Hiramatsu Buhei and given the right to wear swords, as well as a residence in the castle town of Wakamatsu, a Japanese wife and retainers. He is portrayed as wearing a Japanese kimono, overcoat and swords, with Western riding trousers and boots.

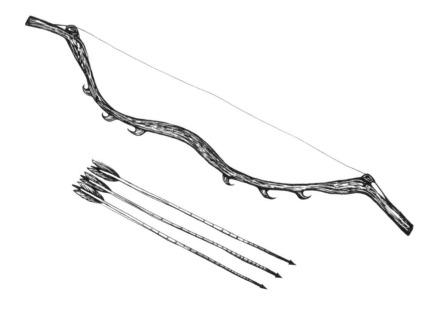

Modern Samurai

1916–2000 *Saburo Sakai*

The legendary Japanese fighter pilot Saburo Sakai was descended from a long line of samurai that had since turned to rural agriculture. His family was intensely proud of their samurai heritage and as Japanese militarism surged in the 1930s, so did the popularity of the old *bushido* ideology. Sakai became the samurai of the skies.

He joined the Imperial Japanese Navy at 16 and later graduated first in his class as a pilot. He was one of the first to test the new A6M2 Zero in combat against the Chinese Air Force and he quickly picked up the art of flying the plane in dogfights. On 8 December 1941, the day after the attack on Pearl Harbor, he flew and attacked a US airbase in the Philippines and shot down his first plane, an American P-40.

If I must die, at least I could go out as a samurai.

He quickly became a fighting ace, but in August 1942, he was hit in the face by a bullet from a Grumman Avenger torpedo bomber. He was blinded in the right eye and his left side was paralysed and he said he was prepared to die. 'I swore I would not go out like a coward, merely diving the plane into the ocean for one bright flash of pain, and then nothing,' he said. 'If I must die, at least I could go out as a samurai. My death would take several of the enemy with me. A ship. I needed a ship.' But he did not find a ship and somehow he made it back over 600 kilometres to his base in New Guinea.

As a result of that injury, Sakai was in the hospital until January 1943. Then he spent a year as an instructor before being transferred to the Yokosuka Wing, based at Iwo Jima, where he flew combat missions again. In one mission 40 Zeros took off and only 20 came back. Sakai was among the group but managed to escape by flying so close to the ocean that his wings dipped in the water several times. He also ignored a kamikaze order and returned after shooting down another Hellcat. He believed a bomber he shot down around the time of Japan's surrender may have been the last American plane downed in the Second World War. He had shot down over 60 planes.

Sakai never lost a wingman in battle, and he managed to bring his aircraft home on over 200 missions, despite the terrible personal wounds he received and the incredible damage inflicted upon his Zero. His popularity increased further after the war due to his humility and his friendly demeanour. He was the ultimate gentlemen and always kept in touch with his old American adversaries – in fact he was dining with US military officers near Tokyo when he suffered a heart attack as he leaned across the table to shake hands. He died later in hospital with the dignity and honour of a modern samurai.

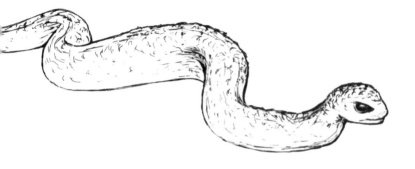

4 | Survival

Jan Baalsrud:
A Timeline of Extraordinary Survival

This story makes *Touching the Void* seem a little like a walk in the park. It's the survival tale of an undercover agent in the Norwegian winter during the Nazi occupation, when German paratroopers were out to kill him at any cost. The 26-year-old Jan Baalsrud found the void, touched it, and then lived in it for months and somehow still survived. But that was only half the story – it took the unquestioning faith and support of over 60 Norwegian families on his journey, who knew that they would be tortured and killed if the Germans ever found out they had helped him.

March 1943 After hard training in the Highlands of Scotland, twelve Norwegian men with the Linge Company (a military unit for agents and saboteurs landing in occupied Norway) go on a mission in a small fishing boat (MS *Brattholm*) to blow up an air-traffic control tower in Tromso in northern Norway.

29 March They come into Toftefjord, some 60 kilometres north of Tromso, and they learn from a local woman that no Germans have ever been there. For good reason, they become uneasy after they accidentally make contact with the wrong shopkeeper, who is not the agent they have been looking for.

30 March Disaster – they must have been reported. They are woken by a German warship in the fjord in the dark and come under immediate fire. They have to abandon ship immediately, so they jump into a little rowing boat and head for shore, rigging the *Brattholm* to explode. Under machine-gun fire and shelling the rowing boat is ripped apart, so they are forced into the freezing water, trying to make it 50 metres to shore.

Jan finds himself in the shallows with his friend Per Blindheim, who is immediately shot in the head and falls. Jan runs through heavy snow towards a hill stretching up 100 metres – he is being shot at but makes it behind a rock and gets his pistol functioning. Four Germans are hot on his tail – one is in Gestapo uniform. He leaps up and shoots the Gestapo officer twice, and then hits one of the other men as well. The other two run for cover.

In the swim, Jan has lost one rubber boot and as he climbs slowly to the top of the hill through the ice and snow he notices a red trail behind him. His big toe has been shot off on his right foot. Ten minutes before, he was asleep on the boat, and now he is alone, the only one to escape – all the other Norwegians have been killed, wounded or captured. He is on a tiny island with a bare foot half blown apart and 50 Germans after him. He keeps running through the rocks and snow and looks back to see the Germans in confusion shooting at shadows.

He has completely lost his bearings and sense of time.

He decides to swim to a rock and then on to another island, Hersoy, in the freezing arctic waters. He is lucky not to die on the way. He is convinced he is about to fall unconscious but he knows the Germans wouldn't suspect he had tried to swim 200 metres. It is chance that washes him ashore on Hersoy, where his limp body twists with freezing cramps.

Jan is found by two rather horrified little girls, whom he soothes by asking their names. Dina and Olaug help him to their mother's house nearby. When Fru Pedersen and Fru Idrupsen find out the wild bandit is Norwegian they take him in immediately, put on the kettle and bring him towels. They give him hot food, a new boot and let him get dry.

31 March	Before light, their eldest son returns and hatches a plan to take Jan to the mainland. He rows Jan to Ringvassoy to a man called Jensen, but he is away, so Jan speaks to Jensen's wife. She is a fearless midwife, who gives him advice about where to go next. He sets off for the south of the island.
1–3 April	The 48-kilometre crossing of the island in winter in deep snow with undulating mountainous and nearly impassable rocks takes four days in heavy boots with no skis. Families along the way let him sleep in their homes for a few hours. He arrives at Bjorneskar to find a contact he has been given called Einar Sorenson. He finds out that his companions have been either shot or tortured to death in Tromso.
4 April	Jan is rowed over the sound to near Tromso by Einar Sorenson and his 72-year-old father, Bernhard. When they reach the mainland, Einar gives him skis and boots to start his journey. The border to neutral Sweden is only 85 kilometres away. He takes refuge at a farmhouse for a long sleep but is too tired to explain himself properly to a Norwegian called Lockertsen, who thinks he is a German deserter. They argue until Jan is finally believed.
5 April	Lockertsen gives Jan a lift in his boat down another fjord to get him in a better position to skirt the mountains on the way to Sweden. Jan lands at Kjosen and puts on his skis. He travels along the first road he sees until there is a road block at Lynseider with a German garrison. Here he goes up a steep hillside to avoid it and crosses barbed-wire fences. Back on the road he presses on only to come round the corner and see 50 or so German soldiers ahead of him, carrying their mess tins from a building to his left. He decides to press ahead and go straight through the middle of them, and to his surprise

they all sleepily get out of his way. Not one of them takes notice of him and in a few seconds he is out of sight.

A few miles later three soldiers standing at a house with papers in their hands see him and give chase. But he is elated, knowing he will outrun them on his skis, his mastery of them taking him up into the mountains and leaving the Germans far behind. He is up in the Lyngen Alps. He climbs to around 1,000 metres as quickly as he can. By 11 a.m. he has made it about 30 kilometres from Kjosen.

At lunchtime a terrible blizzard descends and Jan loses visibility. He knows he will freeze if he stops but he has no idea where he is going. The area is full of steep ravines. Throwing snowballs ahead of him to check whether they land nearby or fall down a drop, he keeps moving for over a day until he has completely lost his bearings and sense of time.

He sleeps under a rock but wakes to find he is trapped in deep gorges and dead-end valleys. Maddeningly, he cannot seem to go down so he has to go up again. On the side of a mountain in the middle of a raging storm, the snow gives way and he falls in a ball, his skis breaking around him, to the bottom of a valley in an avalanche.

Jan falls 100 metres at least. But he is still alive. He comes round to find his head above the snow, so he can breathe, although his body is buried. None of his bones are broken – he has been safely encased – but he has lost his skis, all his food and he has bad concussion. He cannot remember where he is going. He gets out and moves, but the veins in his hands and feet are freezing up, his eyes are blinded by the snow glare and he is hallucinating.

He has now been in the mountains for four days. The snow is so deep he is crawling most of the time. He is going in circles as people who find his tracks can later testify. He begins to shout the names of his dead friends as he carries on into the wall of snow. He comes to some woods and thinks he feels a trapdoor in the snow. The next minute he sees a window in the side of the mountain. Inside he knows there is a warm fire. His mind keeps on playing tricks – he is always just scrabbling at more snow.

But finally he falls headlong into a cabin and onto the floor. This time it is real. It is the home of Marius Gronwald and his sisters. Jan is in a shocking state, a crazed yeti caked in ice with a wild beard and dried blood all over him. His legs and feet are in advanced stages of frostbite.

He cannot say who he is but Marius, a local resistance fighter, suddenly realises he is not a Nazi and must be the escaped Norwegian from Toftefjord. He holds Jan's hand and says, 'If I live, you will live and if they kill you, I will have died to protect you.'

9–15 April Jan lies in Marius's barn recovering from his frostbite and sleeping. The women in the house get the circulation going in his legs but he is an invalid and cannot walk. Any further escape would require a sledge or stretcher. Marius lets three other men in the resistance in on the secret to ask their help in transporting Jan to a safe house in a cabin at Revdal. Jan is too much risk to Marius's family to stay with him. There are Germans looking for him all around the area.

16 April Four men (Alvin Larsen, Amandus Lillevoll, Olaf Lanes and, of course, Marius) carry Jan on a stretcher to the safe house through the deep snow. They wrap him in blankets and give

him a rucksack of food and a paraffin heater to cook with. They pass the German-occupied local school and a sentry post on the way.

At the Savoy Revdal, as Jan calls it, he is comfortable and happy for two days, lying on the bunk in the cabin with food and a stove within reach. He needs his feet to heal enough to allow him to make the last 40 kilometres to Sweden. But they get worse, becoming black and swollen and leaving him in agony. He lies in pain for a further four days, not knowing what to do and convinced he is going to die from blood poisoning.

17–22 April

Marius returns to find Jan delirious and suffering from terrible gangrene. Jan has even been stabbing his toes and feet like a madman in the vain hope of getting some relief. There is blood everywhere.

23 April

The plan is to take Jan up 1,000 metres to a plateau where the resistance in Manndalen are to meet him and take him on further. A special sledge is built for Jan to lie on by the caretaker at the school, right under the noses of the Germans. Then the four men come to attempt this giant mountaineering feat. They are worried the journey will kill Jan. Through brute strength and patience they make it after 14 hours, while Jan falls in and out of consciousness from the pain. But when they reach the plateau there is no sign of the Manndalen men and they search everywhere for their tracks but find none. There is no other option but to dig a hole and leave Jan to cope for himself and wait for the others to come, as there is no way he would survive the trip back. Marius is very downbeat, believing Jan is not strong enough to last a day more in the freezing cold.

23–25 April

The Manndalen men are delayed by the first ever German garrison searching their village and the first expedition finds no sign of Jan. A second party also fails to find him. Then storms come and go until finally Marius hears the devastating news that Jan has not been collected and goes up to fetch his body. Jan has been lying in the snow hole for seven days with a little food and brandy. He has been buried alive by the snowfall but has kept enough space above him to breathe. His ice sarcophagus has kept him warm from the outside blizzard. He has been kept constantly busy: keeping the bottle of brandy upright, wiggling around to prevent frostbite and to ease the pain of the sores all over his back, keeping his sanitation as best he can and avoiding the snow falling in on him all the time. And by this stage he is visualising his own death. So, never a dull moment. Somehow he is still alive when Marius comes back to find him in such a dreadful state. All Marius can do is give him some more food and brandy and leave again.

Two nights later the men from the Manndalen find Jan and try to take him to the border with Finland, but they are delayed by another storm and decide to leave Jan again on the plateau by a rock rather than put him through the pain of more travelling. Unbelievably he lies in this new snow hole for nearly three weeks, although this time he is well stocked with food by the Manndalen, men who come every few days.

The delay lies in convincing the Lapps to transport Jan. They have a very different culture and psychology, rarely expressing opinions about possibilities. As everything has to be certain in their minds, they cannot answer whether they will take Jan across the border or not, because they do not know if they can. This leaves everything at a standstill. However, they are a hardened race that the Germans leave well alone, so their migrating patterns across Scandinavia have complete freedom. They are Jan's greatest hope.

Jan knows the spark within him is now very weak and he starts to worry about wolves. He is sure they have never attacked a man before, but what about a helpless corpse that can't move? He feels very vulnerable. He is finally able to have a look at his feet and it frightens him more. They are frostbitten from the Achilles tendon to the toes, as are his legs all the way to his knees. He is desperate to get rid of the gangrene on his toes so he drinks some brandy, brandishes his penknife and somehow manages to painstakingly cut them all off. The whole grisly operation takes him three days and he feels much cleaner and relieved as a result.

Then one day he hears German voices nearby. He imagines he is hallucinating but when the Manndalen men return they find other tracks. The Germans have been within a few yards of Jan. The men make another vain attempt to move him but the weather closes in again.

Jan is at his wits' end. He is slowly dying every day. He knows the consequences for all the Norwegians helping him if they get caught. He makes up his mind to kill himself. But when he comes to cock his pistol he simply does not have the strength. He cannot even crawl out into the open. He is too weak for suicide.

The Manndalen men realise he is about to die and take him down off the plateau and put him on a bed of birches inside a cave to help his morale. For the first time in weeks he is able to get thoroughly dry. He is in heaven at this feeling and falls into a proper sleep. He sleeps for the best part of four days

23–27 May

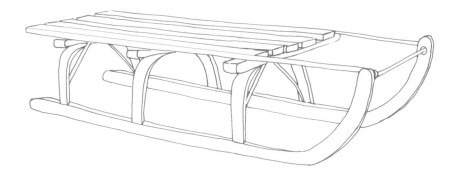

before stunning news arrives that a Lapp has made a firm promise. He is ready to take Jan to Sweden. So Jan is carried up to the plateau by eight men to wait for him.

27 May–1 June Four more long days and nights on the freezing plateau, waiting for the Lapp, then a message comes from Manndalen to say the Lapp is ill and will not be coming. This is the final straw; Jan prepares to lie there and die in the snow – he is too weak to do anything else.

During one of his dreams he thinks he sees a strangely dressed man looking at him for hours and then he realises it really is a Lapp. He says good morning to him but he only hears a grunt back in return.

The next thing he remembers is being surrounded by reindeer, hundreds of them. A couple even come up to have a sniff and he can feel their dank breath on his face. Then two Lapps pick him up without saying anything and put him on a big sledge. They feed him dried reindeer and reindeer milk, cover him in reindeer skins and he is off, tucked in on a sledge in the middle of a herd of reindeer, a huge majestic escort.

They stop in the evening and the Lapps start singing. They come and give him a sip of brandy and offer him more and more through the night. Jan cannot handle more than a sip but they are so keen for him to drink with them that he has to pretend to be asleep. After everything else, he now has to avoid being killed by alcohol poisoning from two drunken Lapps. They drink all though the night but are up early and off again.

It is not too long before they reach Lake Kilpisjarvi by the Swedish border; Jan is excited by the prospect of surviving but they are delayed as the lake ice is melting. Out of the blue they hear gunfire and see a German patrol in the distance. Jan pulls out his pistol, which confuses the Lapps; is this useless specimen trying to defend them or threatening them to go on? There is nothing for it: they set off over the lake towards the border with bullets whistling overhead ...

It is still days before Jan reaches a hospital in Sweden but he is safe from the Germans. He spends a night in a hut with more Lapps and then takes a canoe down a river to a telegraph station, where the operator sends an urgent message to the Swedish Red Cross. An ambulance seaplane picks him up and Jan wakes up after a week in hospital. The doctors ask which surgeon has amputated his toes and Jan clears his throat and says, 'Ah yes, that was me.' His actions had saved his feet. After three months in a ward, his feet and legs are declared safe. He flies back to England in the autumn, elated at the welcome he receives in London but still a little stuck in his private dream and those intense months of survival.

Top Ten Survival Stories

1. Amazon

On Christmas Eve, 1971, German teenager Juliane Koepcke was on a flight with her mother back from Lima, where she went to school, to meet her father in Pucallpa when their plane hit a freak storm over the Amazon and exploded in mid-air. Juliane woke up three hours later strapped into her plane seat in the middle of the jungle. The gods were smiling on her; she had only fractured her collarbone, gashed her right arm and lost vision in one eye. She began looking for her mother, but all she found were empty seats and three women covered in flies. Of the 92 people on board, she was the only survivor.

Dressed in a torn miniskirt and one sandal, she set off through the Amazon, remembering her father's advice to head downhill to get to water, and she soon found a small stream. For nine days the stream provided her with water and a path to civilisation and on the tenth day she found a hut. Hours later a group of Peruvian hunters returned to rescue her. She was alive but in a terrible state – they had to pour kerosene over her to clean out the parasite infestations rife in her skin. She had nearly 40 worms come out of her arms alone, but she was soon reunited with her father.

2. Pocket Knife

While American Aron Ralston was climbing in a canyon in a remote part of Utah in May 2003, a huge boulder fell on his arm and he was trapped. After five days pinned beneath the rock and a long way from civilisation he ran out of food and water. But what he did have was a miserably small pocket knife.

Though most would consider the idea of cutting off their own arm in order to survive inconceivable, it was Ralston's only means of escape. He leveraged the boulder on his arm until all his bones had snapped and then he sawed away at his muscles and tendons. It took a frantic hour of sawing through tendons, ligaments, muscle and bone before he was free and then he had to get down a 30-metre wall before he was found by hikers on his way to his car.

3. Lance Armstrong

The American cyclist is one of the most famous sportsman of all time. He is also one of the most high-profile cancer survivors. In 1996 Armstrong was diagnosed with testicular cancer, which spread to his brain, and yet he remarkably fought his way back to health after being given only weeks to live. He also decided to get back into professional cycling. His will to survive was matched by his will to win. By 2005, in an unprecedented comeback, Armstrong had won seven consecutive Tour de France races (a three-week race over 3,000 kilometres), one of the hardest races in the world to win once. This story has always been overshadowed by allegations that Armstrong used performance-enhancing drugs during his Tour victories – however, this has never been proved and probably stemmed from an endemic drugs culture in cycling at that time and incredulous envy from some rivals and a bitter French press. As he himself has said, he is firstly a cancer survivor and secondly a seven-time Tour de France champion.

4. Desert

Mauro Prosperi, a police officer from Rome, got lost in a sandstorm in the southern Moroccan Sahara during the 1994 ultra-marathon (250 kilometres) race, Marathon des Sables. He wandered several hundred kilometres off-course and survived for the next nine days on boiled urine and the blood of bats whose necks he had wrung. Eventually he found a Tuareg village. He lost over 30 kilograms during his ordeal but returned to Morocco to race six more times.

5. Siberia to India

Slavomir Rawicz was a Polish cavalry officer captured by the Red Army during the German-Soviet partition of Poland in 1939. After being tortured and found guilty at a trial in Moscow, he was sentenced to 25 years' hard labour in a Siberian gulag. After a year in notoriously inhumane conditions, Rawicz escaped in a blizzard with six other prisoners from the camp in Yakutsk. The escapees marched over 6,000 kilometres on foot, across the frozen Siberian tundra, the Gobi desert, through Tibet and over the Himalayas to India. They overcame bitter cold, suffocating heat, thirst, starvation, their own demons and death, as three of the seven died on the way. It took them a year and by the end of his ordeal Slavomir weighed 32 kilograms. Doubt has since been shed on some parts of the story, particularly Rawicz's claim that the party encountered two yetis in the Himalayas.

6. Left for Dead

Big-hearted Aussie Ricky Megee was drugged and left for dead in the middle of Australia's Northern Territory in an area where most people reckon the average mortal would last about four days. The 35-year-old somehow lasted ten weeks.

He was heading to Port Hedland in late January 2006 when he picked up a man on the Buntine Highway. In a hazy recollection of the incident he said the man must have popped something in his drink, for he soon became dazed. He woke up buried in a shallow hole covered in earth and a bit of plastic sheeting being scratched at by dingoes.

He got up to find that his car had been stolen and that he was stuck in the wilderness. He was barefoot but managed to walk for ten days and ate bugs and lizards for survival. He regularly passed out from heat exhaustion until he found some water by a dam.

There he remained for another 61 days, leaving his base once a day to hunt for food. He ate anything he could, including caterpillars, frogs, snakes, leeches and ants. He managed one wasp after removing its stingers and one cockroach, which had him dry-retching for hours. At one point he was forced to remove an excruciating rotten tooth with a piece of wire. He was eventually found by a rancher from a cattle station on the border between the Northern Territory and Western Australia. He was suffering from malnutrition and his body weight had halved to 45 kilograms by the time he was airlifted to the Royal Darwin Hospital.

7. Stoning

In 1997 Zoleykhah Kadkhoda was arrested and charged with adultery within the confines of marriage, an illegal offence in Iran. At the tender age of 20, she was sentenced to death by the magistrate. She was then taken directly and buried to the waist in the ground in her village of Bukan, and a group of locals began stoning her. But the stoning soon elicited outrage from the villagers and they called it to a halt. Kadkhoda was taken to the morgue, seemingly dead, but suddenly started to breathe again and was hurried to hospital. She made a full recovery and an appeal for amnesty was successful. She was soon released.

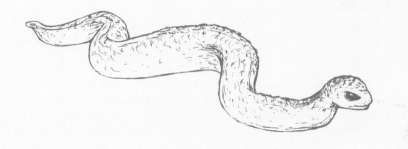

8. Cyclone

In May 1993 a Frenchman, Didier Dahran, was involved in a freak parachuting accident when a cyclone caught him on the descent, spinning him 15,000 metres into the air. After a two-hour whirlwind ordeal, in which his main chute was utterly destroyed, he was eventually spewed out of the cyclone, at which point he took a deep breath and pulled his reserve chute. It still worked and he managed to land safely to tell the tale.

9. Cannibals

In 1846 a group of 87 men, women and children, led by a man named George Donner, set out across the Sierra Nevada Mountains on their way to California. They were forced by the weather to take another route and began to run out of food and water. Many started to die from exposure and starvation. By the time half of them had perished, the others desperately decided to eat the flesh of the dead to survive. The 46 survivors were eventually rescued but were regarded by society as pariahs and criminals for their actions. They were tried and served six months in prison.

10. Bananas

In January 2009, teenager Rudi Alvian was one of a handful to escape an Indonesian ferry disaster after he was kept afloat by a large bunch of bananas in four-metre waves and cyclonic winds. The *Teratai Prima* set sail from Pare-Pare, on the western coast of Sulawesi, for Samarinda, on Borneo, but hit a terrible monsoon, capsized and sank before dawn. Alvian said he would have drowned if he had not found the bananas floating among the debris. He clung to them for over 15 hours, careful not to munch too much of his life raft, until he found a lifeboat. More than 200 people drowned in the disaster. Muhammad Yusuf was also kept afloat by bananas, and another passenger survived by clinging to a long cluster of bamboo.

Ignored in War

If any proof was needed that man has an inner will to survive and the skills to hunt and kill, then it is the story of Poon Lim. Aged 25 at the time, he survived an incredible 133 days alone on the South Pacific, the longest anyone has survived in a similar situation.

The Chinese-born Poon Lim was working as a steward on the British merchant ship SS *Ben Lomond* in 1942 while the Second World War was raging. The boat was on its way from Cape Town to Dutch Guiana when it was torpedoed by a German U-boat on 23 November over 1,000 kilometres east of the Amazon. As the ship was going down Poon Lim grabbed a life jacket and jumped overboard before the ship's boilers blew up.

After two hours afloat in the sea, he found an empty raft with provisions – it had tins of biscuits, a large jug of water, chocolate, some sugar lumps, flares and an electric torch.

Poon Lim kept himself alive by drinking the water and eating the food on the raft, but later resorted to catching rainwater in a tarpaulin and fishing. One cataclysmic setback was that he was a very bad swimmer, so he tied a rope from the boat to his wrist while he kept his strength up by swimming round the raft. He took a wire from the electric torch and made it into a fishhook, and used hemp rope as a fishing line. He also dug a nail out of the boards on the wooden raft and bent it into a hook for larger fish. When he captured a fish, he cut it open with a knife he fashioned out of the biscuit tin and dried the fish on a line over the raft. He also fashioned a fake nest out of seaweed and waited for a gull to land. When it did, Poon struggled with the bird before he killed it and drank its blood to survive.

Even when he saw sharks, he boldly set out to
catch one. He used the remnants of the next
bird he caught as bait. The first
shark to pick up the
taste was only a
few feet long. He
gulped the bait and hit
the line with full force, but Poon
Lim had braided the line to double
thickness and wrapped his hands in canvas
to take the strain. Even so, the shark went for
him when he brought it aboard and he had to hammer
it on the head with the water jug to kill it properly. Then he
cut it open and sucked the blood from its liver to quench
his thirst.

Poon Lim had turned himself from a steward into a special-
forces survivor. But the hardest part was knowing how
tantalisingly close he came to an earlier rescue. A US freighter
saw him but did not pick him up and a US Navy plane dropped
a marker buoy in the water. He was also spotted by a German
U-boat, which had been practising gunnery drills by targeting
seagulls. But despite being in a busy highway of the sea no one
bothered to rescue him because it was wartime. Poor Poon
Lim seemed invisible.

At first he counted the days by tying knots in a rope, but later
decided that there was no point and simply began counting
full moons. On 5 April 1943, Poon Lim reached land and a
river inlet and he was finally rescued by Brazilian fishermen,
who took him to Belem.

During his ordeal, Poon Lim lost over nine kilograms, but was
able to walk unaided upon being rescued. He was the only

survivor from the boat. He spent two weeks in a Brazilian hospital and the British consul arranged for him to return to Britain via Miami and New York. He was awarded the British Empire Medal by King George VI and the Royal Navy even incorporated his tale into a manual on survival techniques.

Making Your Own Luck

Lise Lesèvre

Lesèvre belonged to a hard-line group of the French Resistance in the Second World War when she was arrested by the Gestapo on 13 March 1944 while carrying a letter intended for a Resistance leader code-named Didier.

She had to spend three agonising weeks in interrogation under the direction of Nazi Klaus Barbie. First she was hung up by handcuffs with spikes inside them and beaten with a rubber bar by Barbie and his men. 'Who is Didier? Where is Didier?' were the questions she was asked over and over again.

Next was a bathtub torture. She was ordered to strip naked and get into a tub filled with freezing water. Her legs were tied to a bar across the tub and the Gestapo yanked a chain attached to the bar to pull her underwater:

> During the bathtub torture, I wanted to drink to drown myself quickly. But I wasn't able to do it. I didn't say anything. After 19 days of interrogation, they put me in a cell. They would carry by the bodies of tortured people. With the point of a boot, Barbie would turn their heads to look at their faces, and if he saw someone he believed to be a Jew, he would crush it with his heel.

During her last interrogation, she said, they tied her to a chair and struck her on the back with a spiked ball attached to a chain. It broke her vertebrae.

When she awoke, Barbie was leaning over her, stroking her hands and saying, 'What you have done is magnificent, my dear. Nobody has held on as long as you. It's nearly over now. I'm very upset. But let's finish. Who is Didier?' Lesèvre said nothing. 'I admire you,' he said 'but in the end everybody talks.' But she never did, and she heard him say finally, 'Liquidate her. I don't want to see her any more.'

I wanted to drink to drown myself quickly

She was condemned to death by a German military tribunal for terrorism but was placed in the wrong cell and deported to Ravensbruck concentration camp, where she survived the war. Her husband and son did not. She said they were both deported to death camps when she was arrested.

In 1987, aged 86, she returned to face Barbie in court in Lyon after he had been captured in Bolivia. She recognised him decades later because of his 'pale eyes, extraordinarily mobile, like those of an animal in a cage'. She helped ensure he was sentenced to life imprisonment.

Rufina Amaya

Amaya was a peaceful 38-year-old housewife in 1981 when the Salvadorean army swept through the region of Morazán in a campaign to root out guerrillas and their sympathisers during the civil war then raging in the country.

On 11 December 1981, Rufina was hidden in a tree to which she had run while the soldiers were distracted. She watched and listened as government soldiers raped women, then killed men, women and children by machine-gunning them down and then burned their bodies. Amaya lost not only her neighbours, but her husband, Domingo Claros, whose decapitation she saw, and her nine-year-old son, Cristino, who cried out to her, 'Mama, they're killing me. They've killed my sister. They're going to kill me.' She also lost her daughters María Dolores, María Lilian and María Isabel, aged five years, three years and eight months old. Nearly 1,000 peasants were slaughtered. She was the only survivor.

Following the massacre, people were suspicious of her story despite all she had been through. Amaya became a refugee in Honduras before she returned in 1990 to become a lay pastor for the Roman Catholic Church. Her testimony of the attacks, reported shortly afterwards by two American reporters, was called into question by the US and Salvadorean governments, who were held partly responsible. There was eventually an investigation by a Truth Commission from the UN, which led to the exhumation of the bodies at the site and the conclusion that Amaya's testimony had been accurate.

Great Moments of Bravery

Bob Stuart: Avalanche Survivor

Bob Stuart is a snowboarding instructor with ten years' experience in the Alps. There had been heavy snowfall for two days in Verbier on a Saturday in late February 2006 and many of the high alpine runs were closed. Heavy winds and drifting snow meant there were very dangerous conditions all over the valley. Bob was out with friends off-piste and ducked under some ropes to enable his group to get to an area in the trees where they could take more photos.

He headed over to Bruson, which is just over the valley from Verbier. The backside of the mountain was closed due to avalanche danger. After a morning spent in the trees, the light began to improve and the group set about crossing a certain section of slope that looked as if it might slide, one by one.

'I was number five in the party,' Bob said. 'I followed the tracks that the others had made, making sure I kept inside the already-made tracks. At one point I was travelling very quickly, so I had to shave my speed off a little by turning the nose of my board uphill. This was enough weight to trigger the whole damn mountain. A huge avalanche released and came towards me in seconds. I had no time to think and it took me over 100 metres down the mountain. At first I was able to stay on top, but my board quickly dragged me under and I was sent tumbling into a frightening darkness.

'I was lucky enough to be able to hold my hands around my mouth which gave me an air pocket to breathe. Everything around me was pitch black and I could not move a muscle. I was lying head down with my board above me. The initial feeling was one of overwhelming fear. I thought I was about to die. It was like nothing else I've felt before.

'After the initial shock and realisation that I had just been buried in a huge slide, I knew I had to blank out any fear and emotion and relax as much as I could. The snow from above was slowly crushing my diaphragm so I had to relax my breathing and conserve energy. I knew the other members in the group were not too far away and that they had electronic transceivers on to find me.

'After about eight agonising minutes, I could hear my friends above. I could just about give a muffled scream that helped them to pinpoint my position. They dug me out head first. I had been buried about two metres down. It was a miracle that I had not hit any rocks, cliffs or trees and that I was still alive.

'My friends had been in the right place. The speed of the rescue saved me. If they had gone as far as the forest the rescue time would have been very different and I might well have slipped into unconsciousness.

'The mountain rescue arrived to check that no one else had been buried and we rode down to Le Chable for a few beers. Life seemed quite normal again. I was fine physically and I went out free-riding the next day to get over any fear. To this day I still chat to the lads involved and we all agree that it was one of the best experiences we ever had: we now know to be more careful in the mountains and to take more precautions.'

Survival Myths

Some historical characters are so influential that people simply refuse to believe they are dead. Sometimes the myth of their existence is needed for political reasons or their existence is asserted by the kind of delusional people who go blue in the face arguing for the existence of fairies. There is, of course, nothing intrinsically brave about survival myths, unless the myth just happens to be true. In which case the audacity to disappear and stay in hiding for so long deserves every kind of commendation.

Hitler

There were many conspiracy theorists who thought the charred remains in the Berlin bunker in 1945 were not those of Hitler. Many thought it was a body double and that the Führer had decamped to his Bavarian mountain retreat or somewhere in South America. Stalin even accused the British of secretly holding Hitler captive in a castle in Westphalia. But it suited Stalin to have the figurehead of fascism alive. One set of stories actually argued that Hitler was in hiding at the South Pole, while the increasing paranoia meant that real-life Hitler lookalikes continued to be stopped at customs. The German authorities were rounding up men who resembled Hitler until as late as 1969.

Lord Lucan

This is a mystery which has never been solved. Lucan completely disappeared in 1974 after his children's nanny was found battered to death in his house in Belgravia, London. He was last seen at a friend's place in Uckfield in Sussex later the same night but has not been seen since. Due to a mystery caller, who rang the police to say he heard two gunshots in the grounds of Grants Hill House, in Uckfield, on the night he went missing, many believe his body lies under the ground there. Conjecture persists that a lot of his contacts in the aristocratic world and at the Clermont Club in Mayfair, where he was heavily in debt, may have arranged his disappearance to live in another part of the world.

Elvis

Some vaguely half-sane people claim that 'The King' is still alive and well and has been spotted in various sunny climes around the world. Just after his death, on 16 August 1977, a man calling himself John Burrows, who allegedly bore a startling resemblance to Elvis, was seen buying tickets to Buenos Aires. Elvis had apparently used this pseudonym when travelling, including on one trip to the FBI headquarters in Washington DC. The plot thickens.

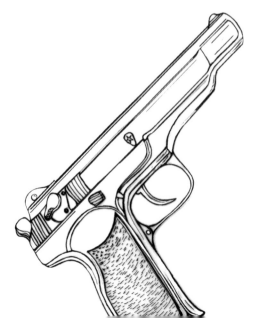

5 | Espionage, Regimes & Revolutionaries

Five Unlikely Secret Agents

Dutch Liberal

The exotically named and resourceful Etta Palm d'Aelders moved to Paris and became courtesan to the French upper classes, managing to pass herself off as a baroness in the eighteenth century. Her revolutionary politics and excellence in the art of pillow talk bought her a position in the French secret service, where she used her wiles to extract information from political thinkers of the time. Etta also continued her feminist work with tireless zeal, delivering a paper to the National Convention, demanding 'the equality of rights without discrimination of sex' and successfully fighting for women's right to divorce. However, her pompous title and liberal mind put her in danger at a time when aristocrats' heads were tumbling at the guillotine. She fled to The Hague and in 1795, when French Revolutionaries invaded the Netherlands, she was shopped for espionage by an old acquaintance in a bid to save his own skin. Etta remained under house arrest until 1798 and died soon after her release.

Brave Act

When the US civil war broke out in 1861, Pauline Cushman was a 28-year-old actress. She was a Southerner by birth who harboured sympathies for the Union government which no one knew about. In 1863, at a performance of *The Seven Sisters* in Louisville, Kentucky, Cushman raised a toast to the Southern Confederate cause and immediately became a heroine. This gave her the ultimate cover when she became a Yankee spy. She was privy to information which she passed on indiscriminately to her contacts in the north and, when she visited the Confederate troops to raise morale she used this as an opportunity to assess their military strategy. Eventually she pushed her luck too far and was discovered with blueprints in the lining of her shoes. She was sentenced to death by hanging; however, she was saved in the nick of time by victorious Union soldiers moving further south.

Identity Crisis

Paul Ernst Fackenheim was a decorated German officer from the First World War who had the misfortune to be a Jew. He was immediately sent to Dachau concentration camp under the Nazis, but in 1941 prisoner No. 26,336 was flabbergasted to be taken off his work detail, referred to as the polite 'Herr' again and dressed in smart civilian clothes. The Nazis needed someone to go on a secret mission into Palestine to unearth the British strategy against Field Marshal Rommel. Moreover, they needed an educated Jew who spoke several languages, including Hebrew. So they decided to train Fackenheim in the art of espionage: how to operate a suitcase-sized radio set, write with secret ink and identify British tanks, airplanes and unit insignias. He was assigned the code name Paul Koch. But on his mission there was a further twist. Fackenheim became a tool of the infighting German intelligence agency and the British were informed that a high-powered SS officer called Obergruppenführer Erich Koch would be landing to spark an Arab uprising.

The British were waiting for a bemused Fackenheim when he made his jump and he was soon picked up and arrested. The British, of course, did not believe he was a Jew recruited for the mission and thought it was a cover story for the SS general. They interrogated him in a jail outside Cairo and sentenced him to be shot after the trial. But at the last moment, the Irish lawyer who had been appointed to defend him located an elderly Jewish woman living in Haifa who

testified that she had known Paul Fackenheim and his parents in Germany. The charges were dismissed and Fackenheim survived the war in a British internment camp.

Matron Mole

Julia Pirie was a petite spinster with a matronly appearance who spent two decades as a lethally efficient MI5 agent. She was recruited to gain access to the Communist Party of Great Britain at the beginning of the 1950s and the unflappable Pirie infiltrated the party as the personal assistant to the party's general secretary.

Her unassuming demeanour masked a rigorous intellect and enormous powers of observation. She compiled reports and photocopied documents, which she passed to her MI5 handlers over a Pimms during cricket matches at the Oval. She also passed on priceless information from her numerous trips behind the Iron Curtain. She was told to resign from her party post in the 1970s and went on to collect intelligence on the Provisional IRA during several missions in Europe.

CIA-trained Tibetans

In alliance with Tibet, fighting against Chinese communism, the US built a top-secret facility at Camp Hale, Colorado, former home of the US Army's Tenth Mountain Division, to train Tibetans to fight against the Chinese in the early 1960s. The Tibetans proved to be incredibly tough and when their espionage training was complete the CIA then dropped them on missions into occupied Tibet and China with personal weapons, wireless sets and cyanide capsules strapped to their left wrists. One such agent, Bhusang, was parachuted into Markham in eastern Tibet in 1961 on a mission with six others. After arming the local resistance, they almost immediately came under attack and fought running battles against the Chinese until they were surrounded. The only survivor was Bhusang. Before he could swallow his cyanide capsule a blow from behind knocked him out cold. He spent the next 18 years in a Chinese prison, where he was tortured and starved until he revealed his training by the Americans and the identities of those taught with him.

Two Regime-Toppling Seductresses

'Well-behaved women seldom make history.'

LAUREL THATCHER ULRICH

Cleopatra

Such is the female aura of the ancient Egyptian queen that her powers of seduction are legendary even today and endlessly replayed in literature and film, from Shakespeare's *Antony and Cleopatra* to the twentieth-century Hollywood blockbuster starring Elizabeth Taylor. Though Helen may have had the face that launched a thousand ships and caused the sacking of the ancient city of Troy, it is the exotic allure and feminine machinations of Cleopatra that stand out over the course of time.

There's not an ambitious girl alive who has not dreamed of living a life like Cleopatra's. During a time when Roman women were not even granted citizenship she was an unheard-of enigma, a powerful and progressive woman who used both her sexuality and her intelligence to get her way in politics hundreds of years before most women could do so again.

Cleopatra has always been regarded as a great beauty, but coins found from the era and an excerpt from Roman historian Plutarch in his *Life of Antony* point to a more alluring character:

> For her actual beauty, it is said, was not in itself so remarkable that none could be compared with her, or that no one could see her without being struck by it, but the contact of her presence, if you lived with her, was irresistible; the attraction of her person, joining with the charm of her conversation, and the character that attended all she said or did, was something bewitching. It was a pleasure merely to hear the sound of her voice, with which, like an instrument of many strings, she could pass from one language to another.

In 51 BC the 18-year-old Cleopatra and her brother, the 12-year-old Ptolemy XIII, became joint rulers of Egypt. Although Cleopatra was married to her young brother, as was the tradition in Egypt at the time, she quickly showed her precociousness by trying to take over on her own; however, a band of courtiers loyal to her brother soon sent her into exile.

It was not long after that Cleopatra succceeded in ingratiating herself with Julius Caesar, in stark contrast to her brother, who had enraged Caesar by assassinating the Roman leader's estranged but well-connected ally, Pompey.

The legend of her first meeting with Caesar involved a Persian rug. When it was unrolled she was revealed wearing a stunningly sensual array of clothes and make-up in a scene which must have been akin to the Ursula Andress white-bikini moment in the Bond film *Dr No*. That night, as the myth goes, Caesar became her lover. And she knew how to keep him keen. When Caesar was most seeking her attention, she would withdraw and leave him wondering what he had done wrong. She had the man who was 30 years her senior and ruler of the western world utterly smitten. Nine months after their first meeting, Cleopatra gave birth. Caesar abandoned any plans to subjugate Egypt and restored Cleopatra to her throne, with another younger brother, Ptolemy XIV, as new co-ruler. *Fait accompli.*

But on 15 March 44 BC Caesar was assassinated.

Unperturbed, Cleopatra was soon back in action. In 42 BC Mark Antony, one of the three pillars of the triumvirate now ruling Rome after Caesar's death, summoned Cleopatra to a meeting. Cleopatra

All she said or did was something bewitching

arrived with huge pomp and ceremony, now a confident woman rather than a flirtatious girl. She so charmed Antony that he chose to spend the winter of 41–40 BC with her in Alexandria, and she eventually gave birth to two children by him.

Four years later, in 37 BC, Antony visited Alexandria and was lured back into Cleopatra's enticing web. This time for good. When it came to types of flattery, as Plutarch said, 'Cleopatra had a thousand. Were Antony serious or disposed to mirth, she had at any moment some new delight or charm to meet his wishes. She played at dice with him, drank with him, hunted with him; and when he exercised in arms, she was there to see.'

Cleopatra also enjoyed winning the odd flutter at his expense. At one of the lavish dinners with Antony, she playfully wagered that she could spend ten million sesterces on one evening meal. He accepted, guffawing. The next night, she had an unspectacular meal served and Antony was playfully scoffing her claim when she ordered the second course –

a single cup of strong vinegar. She then removed a priceless pearl earring, plopped it into the cup, allowed it to dissolve, and nonchalantly drank the mixture.

He was too in love with her to leave again and Alexandria became his home. Cleopatra persuaded him to marry her, though he was already married to Octavia, the sister of Octavian, his fellow triumvir.

In 34 BC Cleopatra and Caesarion (her son by Caesar) were crowned co-rulers of Egypt and Cyprus. Alongside Antony she was also scheming a war against Rome to establish herself as empress of the world. Her ambition knew no limits.

It is hard to imagine how much all this outraged Octavian and the Romans. Unsurprisingly he furiously waged war against Egypt and in 31 BC Antony's forces faced the Romans in a naval battle at Actium. Cleopatra was present with a fleet of her own. When she saw that Antony's ships were losing she took flight and Antony abandoned the battle to follow her. Octavian invaded Egypt and Antony's armies deserted him.

It was over. Cleopatra finally faced ruin. She had outreached herself by taking on the might of Rome. But now she bowed out with grace. Anthony fell on his sword and, rather than accept the ignominy of defeat and be paraded in disgrace as a prisoner, Cleopatra put a deadly snake to her arm.

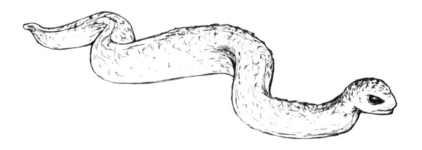

Wallis Simpson

The greatest seduction scandal of the twentieth century was also perhaps its greatest love story. Regarded by some as a libidinous temptress with unlimited ambition and by others as an empowered and modern woman, the American Wallis Simpson changed the history of the British monarchy in quite extraordinary fashion after she met Edward Windsor in 1930.

Though previous kings had been deposed, no king in British history had voluntarily given up his throne before. Simpson was perceived by many in the British Empire as a woman of 'limitless ambition' who was pursuing the King because of his wealth and position whereas in America she was named Woman of the Year by *Time* magazine. She would be 'rising higher' than any American woman had before under the very noses of British aristocratic society.

Wallis was not a classic beauty but she exuded self-confidence and charisma, and had a firm belief in her own attractiveness to men. Elegant and well dressed but harsh in countenance, she was undoubtedly a tough cookie. As a child, she was probably the kind of little girl who had adults wrapped around her little finger and happily tugged the pigtails of the other girls to get what she wanted.

Wallis, who hailed from Baltimore, Maryland, where her mother ran a boarding house, married her first husband, Earl Winfield Spencer, in 1916 when she was 20 years old. A naval pilot, Spencer was a reckless alcoholic and Wallace had affairs with an Argentine diplomat and Mussolini's future son-in-law. She divorced Spencer to marry the easy-going Ernest Aldrich Simpson, who was half-English and half-American. Through a friend, Wallis met Lady Thelma Furness, who in turn introduced her to the Prince of Wales in 1930.

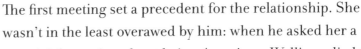

The first meeting set a precedent for the relationship. She wasn't in the least overawed by him: when he asked her a trivial question about being American, Wallis replied that she'd been asked the same thing by every English person she'd met. She said she would have hoped for more originality from the Prince of Wales. In December 1933, while Lady Furness was away in New York, Wallis became the Prince's mistress. By 1934 he was besotted with her, finding her domineering manner and abrasive irreverence towards his position appealing; in the words of his official biographer, he became 'slavishly dependent' on her.

Special Branch detectives started trailing Wallis through London high society in an attempt to discover more about the woman who had captured the Prince of Wales's affections. In 1935, they reported that Wallis was also secretly having a love affair with Guy Marcus Trundle, an engineer who was said to be employed by the Ford Motor Company but who could have been working for British intelligence.

On 20 January 1936, George V died and Edward ascended to the throne as Edward VIII. But the British Empire was dangling on a thread as far as its monarch was concerned. An American *femme fatale* held all the cards.

Her relationship with the King had become public knowledge in the UK by December 1936, and Wallis decided to flee the country as the scandal broke, being driven to the south of France in a dramatic race to outrun the press in an ominous foreboding of what later happened to Princess Diana.

The King then consulted with Prime Minister Stanley Baldwin on the possibilities of marrying Wallis and keeping the crown. The King suggested a morganatic marriage, where he would remain king but Wallis would not be queen, but this was rejected by Baldwin and the prime ministers of Australia and South Africa. If the King were to marry Wallis against Baldwin's advice, the government would be required to resign, causing a constitutional crisis.

It was not seen as very British to put love before duty. They were denied the privacy and peace any couple deserves by the formality of the times. It was all unprecedented. A few days before the abdication, Wallis signed a paper saying that 'she has abandoned any interest in marrying His Majesty'. But it was too late – Edward signed the Instrument of Abdication on 10 December 1936. Wallis's great seduction was complete. Edward had sacrificed his kingdom for his love. Edward said, 'I have found it impossible to carry the heavy burden of responsibility, and to discharge my duties as king as I would wish to do, without the help and support of the woman I love.'

The Duke and Duchess of Windsor were married in June of 1937, in France. But controversy continued to surround them. In the same year they visited Germany as guests of Nazi leader Adolf Hitler and suspicion grew that Wallis might be a German agent after there were FBI reports that she had been having another affair with Nazi Joachim von Ribbentrop and passing him information.

During the war, the Duke was appointed governor of the Bahamas, which Wallis snipingly called 'our St Helena' in reference to Napoleon's exile. They spent the rest of their lives together between a home in Paris and an apartment in New York. But it all seemed a little purposeless, settling into idleness as part of the international jet set and a vacuous life of endless parties. Wallis was allowed to return to the UK for Edward's funeral in 1972. She survived him by 13 years, living alone in Paris, and was quoted as saying, 'You have no idea how hard it is to live out a great romance.'

Timeless Revolutionary

It is hard to say who exactly the real Ernesto 'Che' Guevara was. He is the quintessential twentieth-century radical and becomes more iconic as time goes by. His familiar face looms out from T-shirts, key rings and coffee mugs with more frequency than almost any other world figure.

Whatever your view on his doctrine, methods and cross-boundary idealism, it is certain that his force of will knew no limits. He is still an icon for radical youth and for the marginalised of every society. The life of the Argentinian doctor who left his profession and set out to emancipate the world has been incredibly well documented so I will not try to recount it in detail here. But it was impossible to leave him out of a book on bravery. He was not a *mañana* man.

Five Facets of Che

When Che was a young medical student he travelled throughout Latin America and was so transformed by the amount of poverty he saw he was inspired to rebel against his own background and become a revolutionary. He blamed imperialism and capitalism as the source of the world's woes and unequal distribution of wealth. Eventually he became involved with Guatemala's President Jacob Árbenz Guzmán, and together he and Guzmán began to instigate social reforms.

In 1956 he crossed the Caribbean with Fidel Castro and a handful of other revolutionaries in a yacht called *Granma* and invaded Cuba. He landed in a swamp and fought his way to the Sierra Maestra. He showed such bravery as a freedom fighter (often outnumbered more than ten to one) that he was promoted to *comandante* and two years of guerilla warfare later they ousted the US-backed dictator Fulgencio Batista and installed Castro in his place. Che was immediately hailed as a world liberator from US oppression and dubbed as 'Castro's brain'.

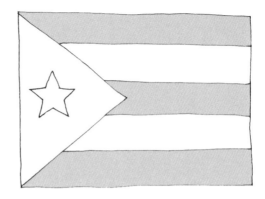

Che was driven by moral rather than material ambitions but he always stuck rigidly to his doctrines and was a notorious disciplinarian. He had no hesitation in sentencing defectors or war criminals to death without trial. His beliefs were not open to compromise.

He was a prolific writer and diarist, composing a manual on the theory and practice of guerrilla warfare, along with numerous books on politics, philosophy and revolution, and an acclaimed memoir about his motorcycle journey across South America, which has been made into a film.

He continued his moral crusade around the world: he addressed the United Nations and spoke against South Africa's apartheid and left Cuba in 1965 to incite revolutions – first in an unsuccessful attempt in the Congo and later in Bolivia. He was captured and executed in Vallegrande in 1967 with the help of the CIA. It was reported that his hands had been hacked off. He was only 39. Fidel Castro delivered a eulogy to nearly a million people, proclaiming that Che's life-long struggle against imperialism and his ideals would inspire future generations of revolutionaries. Castro professed that Che's murderers would be disappointed when they realised that 'the art to which he dedicated his life and intelligence cannot die'.

Bravest Job in the World

Being president of the United States is more dangerous than ever. Though it is undoubtedly something that the forty-fourth American president, Barack Obama, will take in his stride, the job comes with the knowledge that there is no greater assassination target in the world. It already seems clear that Obama is a people's president and likes to mingle on the ground. But as his security know only too well, there have been 90 recorded assassination attempts on US presidents. Being the president or protecting him is not for the faint-hearted. The logistics of security are mind-boggling.

Secret Service
After the assassination of President William McKinley in 1901, Congress directed the US Secret Service to protect the president, a dictate that remains one of its key missions. It employs approximately 3,200 special agents, 1,300 uniformed division officers and more than 2,000 other technical, professional and administrative support personnel.

Air Force One
This is the familiar call sign of any US Air Force aircraft carrying the president. In practice, however, Air Force One is used to refer to one of two customised Boeing 747-200B-series aircraft – among the most recognisable symbols of the US presidency. To many it epitomises state-of-the-art security. It has an unlimited range as it can refuel in midair and the onboard electronics are hardened to protect against an electromagnetic pulse. The plane also had armour-plated wings capable of withstanding a nuclear explosion from the ground and the equipment to jam enemy radar. It is fitted with

the most up-to-date communications, allowing the aircraft to become a mobile command centre in the event of an attack on the US.

Inside, the president and his entourage enjoy 372 square metres of floor space on three levels, including an extensive suite for the president that features a large office, lavatory and conference room. Air Force One includes a medical suite that can function as an operating room, and a doctor is

It is fitted with a night-vision camera, pump-action shotguns and bottles of the president's blood…

permanently on board. The plane's kitchens can turn out nosh for 100 people at a time. There is no billiard room.

Marine One

This is the call sign of any Marine Corps aircraft carrying the president, which is usually a helicopter operated by the HMX-1 'Nighthawks' squadron – either the VH-3D or the VH-60N White Hawk helicopter. Marine Corps aircraft carrying the president's family have the call sign Marine One Foxtrot.

Marine One is often the preferred alternative to a long motorcade. More than 800 marines supervise the operation of the Marine One fleet. As a security measure, Marine One always flies in a group with other identical helicopters to serve as decoys. Television broadcasters are prohibited from airing live footage of Marine One while it is in the air over the White House.

Marine One is reportedly equipped with standard military anti-missile countermeasures and it is always transported (as is the limousine Cadillac One) wherever the president travels, within the US as well as overseas.

Cadillac One, or 'The Beast'

When the president travels out of town it is normally in a motorcade of at least 35 vehicles. Although he sometimes travels in one of two Chevrolet Suburbans, the big mamma of protection is the $300,000 presidential limousine maintained by the Secret Service and known as 'The Beast'. It is fitted with a night-vision camera, reinforced steel plating, tear-gas cannons, oxygen tanks, pump-action shotguns and bottles of the president's blood.

It has an armour-plated body and doors, a raised roof, and boasts a titanium and ceramic superstructure. The car can seat seven people, and includes a communications centre. The sealed interior forms a panic room capable of shielding the president from a chemical-weapons attack and where, were he so inclined, he could probably smoke a cigar and enjoy a foot spa. Even the armoured petrol tank is filled with foam to prevent explosion should it suffer a direct hit, and the tyres allow the vehicle to keep driving even if they have been punctured.

Split Seconds of Bravery

A moment of diplomatic bravery classically understated by the British Foreign Office occurred in the aftermath of a tragic incident in the Gaza strip. On 11 April 2003 peace activist Tom Hurndall was shot in the head by an Israeli sniper as he tried to rescue children scared by shooting in Rafah refugee camp. He fell into a coma and died nine months later.

On 5 May 2003 two armoured Range Rovers with diplomatic plates were transporting his grieving parents and younger brother to see where Tom had been shot when they approached a checkpoint and sentry pillbox manned by Israeli soldiers. It should have been a routine pass but for some reason the Israelis fired a warning shot to stop the convoy.

It must have been a terrible moment for the Hurndall family, who would have wondered if their lives too were now at risk.

But after the cars stopped, the political attaché Andrew Whittaker stepped out of his vehicle with his hands in the air and walked towards the Israeli soldiers with their guns trained on him while the defence attaché, Colonel Tom Fitzalan Howard, phoned the army for an explanation.

Whittaker said: 'My priority was always to look after the family and staff I had in the cars. I knew we didn't want to be sitting in the middle of the checkpoint for any length of time, and that if we tried to drive on we would be in danger of the soldiers mis-interpreting our actions. I also knew that we had to communicate directly with the soldiers, and that trying to do that whilst still in the car was practically impossible (you can't roll down the windows on an armoured Range Rover). So that only really left one option. As I got out of the car I was focused on moving slowly, and ensuring my hands were visible so the soldiers would know there was no threat to them.'

Whittaker stood outside the car for several minutes, waiting, until a hand emerged from the pillbox where the rifle fire had come from, and waved them on.

Tom Hurndall's father said, 'The political officer from Jerusalem [Whittaker] bravely got out of the car and put his hands on his head not knowing whether or not they viewed us as hostile. [He stayed there] until we were waved through.'

Ten US Presidents who Survived Assassination Attempts

1. Andrew Jackson

30 January 1835: An insane house painter called Richard Lawrence fired two flintlock pistols at President Andrew Jackson outside the Capitol building. They both misfired, one from five metres away and the other from point-blank range. Jackson resolutely beat Lawrence with his cane before he was arrested and confined to a mental institution.

2. Theodore Roosevelt

13 October 1912: John F Schrank, a saloon owner from New York, shot Roosevelt with a .38-calibre revolver. By merry providence a 50-page speech in Roosevelt's breast pocket and a metal glasses case slowed the bullet. The stoic Roosevelt exclaimed, 'Quiet! I've been shot', but, much to the frayed nerves of everyone, insisted on giving the bumper speech with the bullet still lodged inside him. He later went to the hospital, but the bullet was never removed. Schrank was found legally insane and was institutionalised until his death in 1943.

3. Franklin D Roosevelt

15 February 1933: Giuseppe Zangara fired five shots at Roosevelt in Miami. Four people were wounded and Chicago mayor Anton Cermak was killed. Zangara, who undoubtedly had mafia connections, was found guilty of murder and was executed. Many believe Cermak was actually the target that day, as the mayor was hot on the trail of Al Capone's Chicago mob.

4. Harry S Truman

1 November 1950: Puerto Rican independence activists tried to shoot Truman while he was staying at Blair House in Washington, and a violent gun battle ensued on the front steps between the assassins and the Secret Service, resulting in the deaths of Secret Service agent Leslie Coffelt and one of the assassins, Griselio Torresola. Truman, who was inside the building, ducked down and was not harmed.

5. Richard Nixon

22 February 1974: Rather eerily, Samuel Byck planned to kill Nixon by crashing an airliner into the White House. Once on the plane, he was informed that it could not take off with the wheel blocks still in place. Hit by the definitive stumbling block, he shot the pilot and co-pilot before killing himself.

6. Gerald Ford

22 September 1975: Sara Jane Moore fired a revolver at Ford from 15 metres away in San Francisco, but a bystander, one Oliver

Sipple, grabbed her arm and the shot went wayward. Moore was sentenced to life in prison but was paroled after 30 years in December 2007.

7. Ronald Reagan

30 March 1981: This was a very close shave. John Hinckley, Jr opened fire when the president was returning to his limousine, following a speaking engagement at the Hilton in Washington. Reagan, his White House press secretary, James Brady, Secret Service agent Tim McCarthy and DC police officer Thomas Delahanty were all shot. They all survived, though Reagan had to have emergency surgery and Brady was permanently disabled.

8. George H W Bush

13 April 1993: A group of terrorists under the likely orders of the Saddam Hussein regime in Iraq were caught by the Kuwaiti military trying to smuggle a car bomb into their country and blow up the US president, who was giving a speech at Kuwait University.

9. Bill Clinton

29 October 1994: Francisco Martin Duran fired 30 shots with a semi-automatic rifle at the White House from a fence overlooking the north lawn, aiming at a group of men in dark suits, one of whom he hoped was Clinton. But the president was in the White House, relaxing to a televised football game when the tackle of the day was going on outside. Courageous tourist Harry Rakosky threw himself at Duran and brought him down before he could injure anyone. Duran was found to have a suicide note in his pocket and was sentenced to 40 years in prison.

10. George W Bush

10 May 2005: One of the assassination attempts on Bush happened when he was giving a speech in Freedom Square in Tbilisi, Georgia. Vladimir Arutyunian threw a live hand grenade towards the podium. Its pin was pulled, but it did not explode because a red tartan handkerchief was wrapped around the grenade to disguise it and somehow kept the firing pin from deploying. Arutyunian was arrested in July 2005, and killed an Interior Ministry agent while resisting arrest. He received a life sentence in 2006.

The first question which you will ask and which I must try to answer is this, 'What is the use of climbing Mount Everest?' and my answer must at once be, 'It is no use.' There is not the slightest prospect of any gain whatsoever. Oh, we may learn a little about the behaviour of the human body at high altitudes, and possibly medical men may turn our observation to some account for the purposes of aviation. But otherwise nothing will come of it. We shall not bring back a single bit of gold or silver, not a gem, nor any coal or iron. We shall not find a single foot of earth that can be planted with crops to raise food. It's no use. So, if you cannot understand that there is something in man which responds to the challenge of this mountain and goes out to meet it, that the struggle is the struggle of life itself upward and forever upward, then you won't see why we go. What we get from this adventure is just sheer joy. And joy is, after all, the end of life. We do not live to eat and make money. We eat and make money to be able to enjoy life. That is what life means and what life is for.

GEORGE LEIGH MALLORY (NEW YORK, 1922),
THE ENGLISHMAN WHO DIED ON MOUNT EVEREST IN 1924.

6 | Exploration

Serendipity: Five Accidental Land Discoveries

Canada
Leif Ericson, a Viking, was blown off course past Greenland around the year 1001 and was probably the first European to land in North America. He established a settlement at Vinland, now believed to be the northern tip of Newfoundland in Canada.

Brazil
In 1499, Vincente Pinzon was trying to find more of the West Indies, some of which he and Columbus had already discovered. Instead, he stumbled across the coast of Brazil, in the north-east region now known as Cabo de Santo Agostinho in the state of Pernambuco.

Galapagos
The bishop of Panama, Fray Tomas de Berlanga, was no gung-ho explorer. In 1535 he was sailing to Peru, recently conquered by fellow Spaniard Pizarro, when his ship was becalmed and carried west by currents to the Galapagos. He landed but saw painfully little value in the islands, claiming they were dross and worthless.

Bermuda
Admiral Sir George Somers set sail from Plymouth, England for Jamestown, Virginia in 1609, carrying around 600 people, many of whom were settlers bound for the New World. But in late July they ran into a hurricane and Somers himself took the helm to fight the winds. The ship began to leak and sink but on 28 July Somers spotted land. They were saved. The whole crew was beyond the point of exhaustion and the hold was full of water. It was a very lucky break. They had landed

on Bermuda, also known as the Somers Isles, where Sir
George founded a successful colony in a veritable Eden.

Australia

The Dutch sailor Dirk Hartog was following a route to the East
Indies in 1616 when he turned north considerably too late
and sighted 'different islands' off the coast of western
Australia, near Shark Bay. Hartog stepped ashore on 25
October 1616, the first recorded landing by a European on
Western Australian soil.

A Swiss Family Robinson of Explorers

Father of Geography

Alexander von Humboldt was not just a charismatic German
explorer, he was truly a man who makes bees look idle. He
was a scientist, a botanist and one of the fathers of modern
geography. He was a serious explorer who went to South
America between 1799 and 1804 and described it from a
scientific point of view for the first time. He wrote extensively of
his findings, filling a set of volumes over the course of 21 years.

It was under the patronage of the Spanish minister Don
Mariano Luis de Urquijo that von Humboldt decided to make
Spanish America the scene of his explorations, and he
rewarded his patron with a smorgasbord of colourful
discovery. After landing at Cumana, Venezuela, he found the

'oil-bird', which he named *Steatornis caripensis*, and he witnessed and documented a remarkable meteor shower. He then set out to explore the course of the Orinoco river.

He covered 2,776 kilometres of wild and largely uninhabited country. He found the place where the Orinoco and the Amazon conjoined and captured electric eels, receiving dangerous electric shocks when he investigated the sparky critters.

Without taking a breath, he visited Cuba, where he compiled statistics on the population and geology before he headed to Quito, Ecuador, on 6 January 1802. Here he nonchalantly climbed Pichincha and Chimborazo, where his party reached an altitude of 5,878 metres, a world record at the time. He also observed the transit of Mercury and studied the fertilisation properties of guano, the use of which was then introduced to Europe with great success.

Forest Mother

The British artist Margaret Mee was known as the Mother Theresa of the rainforests. She began her Amazonian journeys in 1956 when she was 47, and spent the best part of 30 years travelling through humid tributaries in a small dugout canoe and living for weeks on end with the Tucano indians. She braved stifling heat, sickness, rapids and even held off drunken prospectors with a revolver. She painstakingly observed and painted native plants in their natural habitat and discovered several unknown species that now bear her name. She completed 15 expeditions while she lived in Sao Paolo, where she would teach in between her travels.

She painted during a time of disastrous change. In the 1960s, Brazil built the Trans-Amazonian Highway and opened the area to farming, ranching, mining and hydroelectric projects. Mee was one of the first to speak out against the deforestation that led to such massive destruction during the 1970s and 1980s and which, by a sad twist of fate, made her work all the more valuable. Scientifically, no equivalent record of Amazonian plants has ever been created. Her remarkable watercolours include the only known records of certain plants, many of which may now be extinct.

At the age of 79 she was still keen to return to the Amazon but died in a car crash in England, leaving behind a botanical legacy.

Tree Doctor

Just when you thought there were few untouched places left to explore, enter Dr Stephen Sillett, tree climber. Sillet is the world's foremost expert on tall trees and forest-canopy exploration. The American, who was born in 1968, was the first scientist to enter the redwood canopy and pioneer new climbing methods.

To reach the tops of the trees, Sillett fires an arrow to set a climbing line and hauls himself up using a safety swing. Once ensconced in the canopy, the nimble-limbed Sillett gracefully moves in a style known as skywalking using pulleys within a web of climbing ropes, and to reach tricky distant branches he deploys a Tyrolean traverse. He has studied and climbed tall tree species in the USA, Canada and Australia.

Fossil Hunter

The final member of this Family Robinson is Sue Hendrickson, a marine archaeologist, adventurer and explorer whose CV reads like an Indiana Jones film. Hendrickson has delved her industrious nose into fossils, artifacts and shipwrecks all over the world, including fossilised whales in the Peruvian desert, 23-million-year-old amber-encased butterflies in the Dominican Republic, ancient Egyptian and Napoleonic treasures deep in the Nile river in Egypt and Chinese porcelain from a 400-year-old sunken Spanish galleon off the coast of the Philippines. In 1990 she made a great fossil find – the most complete Tyrannosaurus Rex in a remote cliff in the Black Hills of Dakota. It took nearly a month to remove the gigantic bones from the ground.

New Levels of Exploration: Mike Horn

There are many tough adventurers in the world today but the South African Mike Horn invariably manages to take it to another level. Some have said he takes it too far. This is the man who body-boarded the whole way down the Amazon river and conquered the North Pole in the freezing darkness of winter, a trip no one ever dreamed of until Horn practically crawled there three years ago, bleeding from every orifice, with the legendary Norwegian polar fiend Borge Ousland. Horn has also crossed the entire Arctic Circle and made it round the world following the equator for 18 months.

At present he is in the middle of the world's greatest ever expedition, which he started at the beginning of 2009 by trekking and kiting nearly 2,000 kilometres for over a month across the Antarctic plateau. Using no motorised power for Pangaea, as the expedition is called, Horn is spending four years travelling to both poles, climbing mountains in the Himalayas, traversing deserts in Asia and Africa, wading through wetlands in Canada and braving the clammy perils of the Amazon jungle once more. He will journey through places as disparate and harsh as Kashmir, Siberia and the Skeleton Coast in Africa.

'This is a trip I have been dreaming about all my life,' Horn said. 'Everything has led here – it's been my ultimate ambition. Being an explorer today is not about records and discoveries any more – it's about taking yourself outside your comfort zone and striving to better yourself and the world around you.

'I am looking to help teach the world through beauty not through fear. The attitude about climate change is over-the-top and doom-mongering – we must learn to appreciate what we have. But gees, the hardship just never changes. In winter you freeze your balls off and in summer you get bitten to death.'

> *People do not get out of their comfort zone enough in life – they never know what they can achieve or what it is like to live in a certain way.*

His only concession is a promise to old friend Johan Rupert not to go over 8,000 metres and enter the death zone in any mountain range on his own. To do so would be like signing a death warrant if even the tiniest thing went wrong.

The organisation and logistics of such an enterprise are like a new science in themselves. Horn has a crew on his expedition boat led by South African skipper Nick and Brazilian doctor Claudio. *Pangaea* is one of the most high-tech custom-made sailboats ever built. From the ice breaker on the front and the navigation system, to the giant TV screen and the mini desalination plant, this boat is capable of withstanding almost any condition.

Back at his office in Switzerland, his wife Cathy and his brother Martin run the huge support operation, recruiting young explorers from around the world, liaising with charitable projects and dealing with the media circus that trails behind Horn but gives him the publicity he and his sponsors need.

Along with the equipment necessary for survival, and success, Horn has developed his body into an efficient machine. 'It's a bit like putting fuel in different cars – one will always go further than another. Put fuel in me and I will always go further.'

He needs to eat round the clock to keep himself going. He starts the day with oatmeal and brown sugar and dried fruit, using melted snow in his stove to cook with. During the day he drinks over a litre of liquid-protein food and munches, more pleasantly, on a day-pack of chocolate, cookies, brownies, nuts and fruit. In the evening he has a choice of freeze-dried chicken curry or beef stroganoff, always mixed with lashings of cooking oil.

He says the Antarctic is a harsh place to exist. 'God, I hate the cold. It's worse now than ever it was. The more you are exposed to the cold, the quicker you get cold each time. My body can really tell when it gets a few degrees colder, which most people would not notice.' The knowledge that he is a human thermometer irks him. 'It's a real pain. I know I won't function so well and I need more fuel.'

His first leg across the Antarctic was measured in calories, not in distance – Horn consumed 8,000 calories a day to keep himself going and slept for two hours at a time because, as he said, 'If I slept for five hours I would use up 5,000 calories.'

He must also keep hydrated at all times and when he wakes up to relieve himself he urinates in a bottle inside his tent. 'I then use the bottle to warm my feet,' he adds with an explorer's chuckle.

He tests and develops his own gear and now prefers old-school breathable wool to modern fabrics. He likes to keep things simple and maintain the ability to mend his skis or his sledge, which weighs in eye-wateringly at over 200 kilograms due to all the food and fuel. He monitors his position with a GPS system and keeps in touch by satellite phone.

He says he learned more from his aborted trip to the North Pole than from any other experience: when his fingers became frostbitten after tying a shoelace he ignored his doctor's advice and decided to carry on. He eventually had to be rescued by a Russian helicopter and lost the tips of two finger and his thumb. 'It was the most amazing lesson of my life,' Horn said.

His next trip was the hellish winter trip to the North Pole. He and Ousland were just pipped by two Russians to be the first to travel to the North Pole in the freezing darkness of winter, even though the Russians had started later and he and Ousland took 30 days less. On this arduous journey, which shocked the world, temperatures were often under minus 60°F. Horn even wore a waterproof trisuit to swim through the water between the ice, 'playing Russian roulette', hoping he wouldn't sink too far.

Then there were the polar bears to deal with. Horn was asleep in the tent one night when he felt a polar bear nuzzling him through the tent material. 'It was sitting in my sledge so I woke up Borge and screamed, "Borge, there's a bear in my sledge, there's a bear in my sledge."

'Borge woke up and said, "Yes Mike, there's a bear in YOUR sledge", and then he went back to sleep.'

But of all the places in the world, Horn prefers the jungle. 'I am happiest [there]. The jungle awakens your senses. It gives you eyes in your feet and ears on your backside. It is where I did my special-forces training. I can survive and swim and live off the land like a monkey and, if I need to, I can eat the monkey.'

It's no safer though. He has been just as close to death in the jungle as he has been at the North Pole. In Colombia, where he was following the equator, he was bitten by a poisonous snake. He felt a little scratch on his finger in the undergrowth and then suddenly started to feel drunk and have trouble with his vision. But he had not seen the snake so did not know what it was. After finding the wound on his finger, and bleeding it as best he could, he went blind. For two days he lay in his hammock, unable to see and with the feeling gone from his face. He said by day four he didn't think there'd be light at the end of the tunnel, but by day five he could see again and walk tentatively.

He also had a run-in with a drugs baron. 'I was hauled out of the water by some guys with guns and led to their boss. He

asked what the hell I was doing there and didn't believe me when I said I was in a kayak on my way round the world by different means. I thought I might be shot. I thought that was it – then I remembered that I had a newspaper article about me going round the Arctic Circle and the guy read it and was utterly bemused.

'He said, "You should not be in this area – you can go through here and carry on but I never want to see you here again or we will kill you."'

But perhaps Horn's most unpleasant encounter was with parasites or worms. He started to see the traces of worms' bodies on his legs and he realised they were gradually creeping up his body. He became so paranoid about it that he marked them with a pen every day. 'Ah, I really did not want them to get to my groin,' he said with a grimaced grin at the memory.

Horn is the second-eldest of four kids and grew up running to school and back every day in Johannesburg. His father, who had been a world-class athlete, died suddenly of stomach cancer at 43, when Horn was 18. His father's parting advice, Horn recounts, was: 'While you're alive, live. Don't live half a life.'

Horn joined South Africa's special forces for a year in 903 Special Service Company and saw action in Angola. A possible rugby career – Horn was scrum-half for the former province of Transvaal – was cut short in a drunken prank at Stellenbosch University when his foot was turned the wrong way round. In 1987, at the age of 21, he decided to give away all his worldly possessions and make a life in Switzerland. Soon after he became known for setting the record for body-boarding down a waterfall, and then for his daring trip down the Amazon.

He met his wife Cathy, a nurse from New Zealand, in 1990 and has said nothing he does would be possible without her backing and the support of his two daughters, Annika and Jessica. 'People think explorers are running away, but we need the love and stability behind us to be successful.'

Horn has never been on a family holiday, though he took both his daughters to the North Pole when they were 12 and 13. Cathy said, 'Life is not easy sometimes, but then when is it ever? We have a very good life.'

But there's a definite dichotomy in Horn between the family man and a man who is so desperate to be alone. He is sincere when he says, 'The first step of my journey is always the best moment, when it's all down to you, and the last step is always an anticlimax because you come back empty, because the adventure is over.'

'I suppose I am religious,' he said. 'When I am out there I feel close to nature, to a higher being. Every adventurer turns to a higher force at some stage. I do believe, but not in Buddha or Mohammed or whoever. I just know that if you see the face of nature you must believe and I do hope I die alone with nature.'

He envies people who get on the Tube and go to work; he doesn't know how people can do it. But he also believes people 'do not get out of their comfort zone enough in life – they never know what they can achieve or what it is like to live in a certain way. As an explorer I am always trying to be comfortable in uncomfortable situations.'

A Day in the Life of...

Alastair Humphreys, around-the-world cyclist

The laid-back young Englishman spent four years going round the world on his bicycle. He cycled 74,000 kilometres on a tiny budget from 2001–5. No day was ever quite the same, as the two books he wrote on his travels testify, but each day brought pain and adventure in equal measure, as his words vividly describe:

❛If you're not hurting you're not riding hard enough. If you're not hungry you've eaten too much. If you're not cold you're carrying too many clothes. If you know you will succeed it's too easy.

Days are long on the road. Pack up and pedal into the dawn. Ride until sunset. It's easy to kill time but you can kill distance only by riding. Roads roll on for ever, linking and connecting and reaching so far ahead that to think about the end is to think of something that feels impossible. So settle for today, for earning the small distance that the day's long hours will allow you. Roads drenched with rain, stinging hail, pulsing heat, slick ice, buffeted by winds on loose gravel, deep sand, tangled rocks, thick snow. Roads of smooth tarmac down mountainsides on sunny days with warm tailwinds and scenes of impossible beauty. Roads furious with traffic through grim slums, bland scrub, concrete jungles, polluted industrial wastelands. Monotony in motion. Roads too hard and too long that break you, expose you, scorn you and would laugh at you if they cared. Roads too hard and too long that you pick yourself up from, have a word with yourself, and make it to an end you once doubted. Roads you have never ridden to places you have never seen and people you have never met. Days end. A different sunset, a different resting point, a different perspective. A little less road waits for you tomorrow. A little more road lies behind you.

Choose your road. Ride it well.❜

Top Five Stubborn Explorers

The Briton Ernest Shackleton was the stubborn type of hero that other explorers are often measured by and the modern versions include, of course, Mike Horn and the Norwegian Borge Ousland, who many explorers rate as the greatest polar adventurer. But there are many others who have shown a similar kind of mettle.

Sun Worshipper

The German explorer Friedrich Gerhard Rohlfs (1831−96) joined the French Foreign Legion as a personal physician to a Moroccan nobleman, before he eventually set off on his own to explore the oases of Morocco. He made his first expedition to the Sahara disguised as a Muslim, but he was attacked and robbed and left for dead, his leg almost severed from his body. He was rescued, but these injuries only made him more determined to see more of the desert.

The pain of the cold on his wounds also kept him from returning to Europe for most of his life. Rohlfs was the first European to cross Africa north to south, entering through the Mediterranean and travelling all the way down to the Gulf of Guinea. He was the second European explorer to visit the region of the Draa river in the south of Morocco.

Don't Write Off an Aussie

This is the second Australian in the book whose relaxed and determined nature has seen him survive an impossible situation in which most would have died. In fact, on 26 May 2006, Lincoln Hall was reported as dead to the world by his expedition party, who had been forced to leave him with altitude sickness near the top of Mount Everest. According to reports, Sherpas attempted a rescue for hours, but as night began to fall, their oxygen supplies diminished and snow blindness set in. They were ordered by their expedition leader, Alexander Abramov, to leave an apparently dead Hall on the mountain and return to camp.

However, the next morning at 7 a.m., Hall was found still alive by a team making a summit attempt. Briton Myles Osborne said, 'Sitting to our left, about two feet from a 10,000-foot drop, was a man. Not dead, not sleeping, but sitting cross-legged, in the process of changing his shirt. He had his down suit unzipped to the waist, his arms out of the sleeves, was wearing no hat, no gloves, no sunglasses, had no oxygen mask, regulator, ice axe, oxygen, no sleeping bag, no mattress, no food nor water bottle. "I imagine you're surprised to see me here," he said. Now, this was a moment of total disbelief to us all. Here was a gentleman, apparently lucid, who had spent the night without oxygen at 8,600 metres, without proper equipment and barely clothed. And alive.'

A huge rescue effort swung into action and Osborne's team, led by American Dan Mazur, abandoned their summit attempt to look after Hall, who was now badly frostbitten and delusional from severe cerebral oedema, while a rescue team of 12 Sherpas climbed up from below. Hall was brought down the mountain, walking the last part of the way to Everest's North Col and in a few days he was back to good health.

Not Quite Collared by the Congo

Described as a full-faced, stubborn, self-willed, uncompromising and pensive fellow, Henry Morton Stanley was a Welsh journalist and explorer famous for his trips into deepest Africa, particularly the *New York Herald*-sponsored expedition in 1817 to find Livingstone. In 1874 the *Herald* and the *Daily Telegraph* financed Stanley on another expedition, this time to uncover the last great mystery of African exploration – tracing the course of the river Congo to the sea. The logistics of this enterprise in the nineteenth century are hard to fathom. They faced heat, disease, starvation and attack, but Stanley forged on to the point of idiocy with all his men dying around him.

Stanley used sectional boats to pass the great cataracts separating the Congo into distinct tracts. After 999 days, on 9 August 1877, Stanley reached a Portuguese outpost at the mouth of the river Congo. Only 114 of the original 356 survived, including the bloody-minded Stanley, who was the only European to survive.

Maverick Frenchman

During the late 1950s, 1960s and early 1970s, René Desmaison became one of the most famous of a superset of elite French climbers who redefined alpinism, along with Lionel Terray, Gaston Rébuffat and Jean Couzy. Desmaison became famous for his brilliance in the mountains but also infamous for his single-mindedness.

In 1966 he was expelled from the world's oldest and most prestigious mountain guiding company, the Compagnie des Guides de Chamonix after leading an 'unsanctioned' rescue of two German climbers trapped on the west face of the Petit Dru.

Then in 1971 he attempted a difficult winter route left of the Walker Spur near Chamonix with the young guide Serge Gousseault. But a mini rock avalanche cut their ropes while they were climbing the face and they became stranded; then Gousseault developed severe frostbite in his hands. When help finally came, after two weeks, Gousseault had been dead for three days, and Desmaison was hallucinating and clinging onto life by sucking on bits of ice. By the time he made it to hospital he was hours from complete renal failure.

Ice Cave

In 1982 Kiwis Mark Inglis and Phil Doole were hit by a blizzard on the slopes of New Zealand's highest mountain, Mount Cook. They built an ice cave and waited for the storm to pass, but it was 13 days until they were rescued. They survived on meagre rations, but their problem was the cold. They lost the circulation in much of their legs, which had to be amputated. But losing their legs hasn't stopped the men's climbing careers. Both went on to summit Mount Cook and Inglis became the first double amputee to conquer Everest.

Exploring Brain and Consciousness

The last great frontier of exploration is not likely to be found in a desert well or on a far-flung iceberg or even in the far reaches of space; it is most likely to be within. The one complex land we still do not understand is the human brain. Our consciousness and subconscious are still a land of conjecture. It's a brave new future for us all.

The Future

One woman who has demystified the science of the human brain is Susan Greenfield, a professor in pharmacology at Oxford University. Here is an extract from one of her lectures theorising about the future. It was given at the University of Kent in 2002:

> No one would deny that in this coming century people are going to end up living healthier and longer lives as everybody gives up smoking, takes up regular exercise, eats brown rice and, with increasing ease, engages in organ transplants – below the neck at least. Clearly we are going to be squaring up to being on this planet for longer.
>
> Moreover, with the advent of all the gizmos that come on to the market to wow us almost daily, we shall have more leisure time.
>
> Most of us feel that there is 'more to life' – some kind of individual fulfilment. I predict, therefore, that we are going to be asking the kinds of questions that were previously restricted to student rooms late at night, or one's teenage years – we shall be looking introspectively at what our purpose is, expecting to be happy. This means that at centre stage will be the one organ that we would not wish to exchange, the brain.

So what will be happening in the future? We can predict that there will be increased monitoring of all the processes that touch on our lives, from the micro to macro. At the molecular level, genetics will play a huge part in determining what may, or may not, be happening in our bodies and brains.

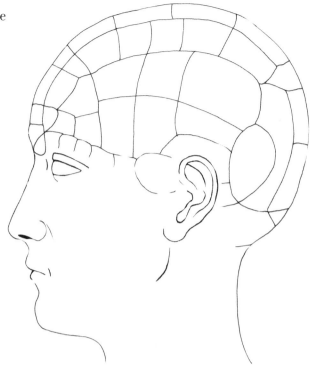

However, it is essential to remember, to be aware of, what this gene technology will, or won't, deliver if we are to start shifting the building blocks of our brain function. We shouldn't kid ourselves that we will have the precision of specific function that is often implied. At the level of cell to cell, interactions will play an important part through an increase in both drugs of abuse and drugs prescribed to treat how we are feeling. As with genes, it is important to realise that you don't have a sophisticated function like happiness or sadness locked in to a single chemical, but it is what that chemical does within the brain to certain configurations, in order to think of ways of avoiding taking drugs but producing the same net effect.

At the next level up, in brain-body processes, scanning, as we have seen, will also be very valuable, but will open up our brain and body processes to the outside world. Nanotechnology will give increased monitoring of the states of our body and perhaps even of our mind, so that we are much more interactive with the outside world and it is more sensitive to us. This raises the interesting question about where one's body ends and the outside world begins as cyberspace starts to transcend the two.

Finally, we have body-environment interactions, where information technology might give us a whole new world of virtual reality – being on the one hand ecologically beneficial, but perhaps, on the other, leading to an increased standardisation and the potential for more manipulation.

Are we going to see, with these new technologies, a manipulation of the individual, social divisiveness according to genome, virtual and designer children and increasing competition to be smarter and more beautiful than the rest? Or are we going to celebrate individuality and have time to develop our own individual potential?

The one big threat that I can see, one that would turn the future into a sunset rather than a sunrise, would be a scientifically illiterate society.

The Golden Age of Spanish Exploration

1492   Christopher Columbus's well-documented voyage to America, the New World, is financed by King Ferdinand and Queen Isabella of Spain. He also discovers Haiti and Jamaica and visits the Dominican Republic, which he names Hispaniola.

1493   The island of Montserrat, in the Caribbean Sea, is named by Columbus after the mountain near Barcelona.

1494   Spain and Portugal claim the lands of the New World in the Treaty of Tordesillas, which split the lands of central South America 370 leagues west of Cape Verde with a line. Spain claimed territories on the west, Portugal on the east.

1496   Spaniards colonise the Dominican Republic. Bartholomew Columbus, brother of Christopher, founds Santo Domingo, which subsequently serves as the capital of all Spanish colonies in South America.

1498   Christopher Columbus lands in Venezuela.

1502   Columbus sails on his fourth and last voyage to the New World (Honduras and Panama) and lands at Cariari, now known as Puerto Limon in Costa Rica. The explorer Rodrigo de Bastidas visits Panama.

1513   Vasco Nunez de Balboa, explorer, crosses the isthmus of Panama and claims the Pacific Ocean for Spain.

1516   Juan Diaz de Solis became the first European to land in Uruguay.

1517   Francisco Hernandez de Cordoba leads an expedition and lands on the Yucatan coast in Mexico.

1519   Conquistador Hernan Cortes founds Vera Cruz in Mexico. Then he enters the Aztec capital Tenochtitlan and captures their king, Montezuma II.

1520s   Conquistador Francisco Pizarro leads several expeditions into Peru.

1523–4 Conquistador Pedro de Alvarado leads an expedition from Mexico and invades Guatemala, landing at El Salvador.

1528   Juan de Zumárraga arrives as bishop of Mexico City and begins native conversion to Catholicism.

1535   Conquistador Francisco Pizarro overthrows the Incan Empire and Ecuador comes under Spanish rule.

1536–8 Conquistador Gonzalo Jiménez de Quesada leads an expedition into the Andes and invades Colombia, obtaining massive amounts of emeralds and gold.

1540   Conquistador Cabeza de Vaca is appointed governor of the Brazilian province of Rio de la Plata.

1541   Pedro de Valdivia begins conquest of Chile and founds Santiago. Francisco de Orellana, one of Gonzalo Pizarro's lieutenants during his 1541 expedition into the South American interior in search of El Dorado, branches out on his own. He discovers the Amazon river, which he names after the fierce female warriors that accost him. In one of the most improbably successful voyages in history, Orellana manages to sail the length of the Amazon, arriving at the river's mouth the following August.

1542   Spain invades and conquers Belize.

1545   The Spanish conquer Bolivia.

1546   A Mayan rebellion in Belize forces the Spanish to leave.

1561   Santa Cruz is founded by Nuflo de Chávez.

1561   Juan de Cavallon leads the first successful colonisation of Costa Rica.

1567   Belize is reconquered.

'Bravery never goes out of fashion.'

William Makepeace Thackery
(nineteenth-century English writer)

The Language
of Bravery

Expressions with Their Roots in Bravery

Bob's Your Uncle

Invaders have found Afghanistan to be a barren and hostile place since the dawn of time. One of the most successful military commanders here was Lord Frederick Roberts, a feared and brutal soldier in the British Raj who forced his way through the Khyber pass in 1878 and captured Kabul by ruthless methods. He butchered Afghans by the hundreds and hung bodies around the streets as a warning to others who might dare to cross him; however, he was so kind and fluffy to his own soldiers that they called him Uncle Bobs. If he were in charge, it was said, it was a bed of roses for his troops, hence 'Bob's your uncle'.

Break a Leg

This popular expression, meaning 'good luck', originated in the theatre and was said to actors before going on stage, although it is now used much more widely. It is thought to date back to John Wilkes Booth, the renowned assassin of US president Abraham Lincoln. After shooting Lincoln, Booth, himself an actor, jumped from the president's box down to the stage and apparently broke his leg when he landed awkwardly in heap. He was considered to be very lucky for escaping the theatre undetected by cunningly crawling out before he could be caught, hence the root of the expression.

Jack the Lad

The exploits of eighteenth-century thief Jack Shepherd, also known as Gentleman Jack, inspired this phrase. Jack escaped from prison five times (even from shackles in solitary confinement) and came to be loved by the public before he was hanged at 22 years old.

C'est magnifique mais ce n'est pas la guerre

Loosely translated as 'It's magnificent alright, but it's hardly cricket', this expression is used to describe something that isn't sensible, especially in battle. It was a comment made by the French general Pierre Bosquet to Sir Austen Layard after the Charge of the Light Brigade at the Battle of Balaclava in 1854, when fewer than 700 British cavalrymen charged valiantly on their horses into a valley surrounded by Russian artillery and riflemen and recorded very heavy losses. As some kind of twisted compliment, even the Russians thought the British soldiers must have been drunk to attempt such an attack.

Chance One's Arm (or Luck)

The Earl of Kildare is said to have sought an ending to a quarrel between his family and the Ormondes at the end of the fifteenth century by sticking his arm through a hole cut in the door of St Patrick's cathedral in Dublin, where the Earl of Ormonde had taken refuge. He did so in the hope they would embrace it rather than chop it off. Fortunately, he was embraced and the feud was ended.

Black Hole of Calcutta

After the East India Company's Fort William was captured during an uprising, the Nawab (ruler) of Bengal incarcerated 146 British prisoners in its tiny prison. The conditions were so cramped and stuffy that only 22 men and women did not suffocate to death. Hence any crowded or cramped dark place is sometimes compared to the Black Hole of Calcutta.

As Game As Ned Kelly

This refers to the daring nature of nineteenth-century Australian desperado and bushranger Ned Kelly, who had a

When you go up to the mountain too often, you will eventually encounter the tiger. (Chinese)

Fear is only as deep as the mind allows. (Japanese)

Bravery without intelligence is not bravery. (Arab)

He who risks nothing has nothing. (French)

True bravery is without witness. (American)

One brave man is equal to 100 cowards. (Pathan – eastern Afghanistan)

A brave man is scared of a lion three times: first when he sees the tracks; second when he hears the first roar; and third when they are face to face. (Somali)

A brave man will face a situation no matter how dreadful. (Filipino)

All are brave when the enemy flies. (Italian)

popular career in crime before he was finally captured in a self-made suit of armour after a massive shoot-out and hanged from the gallows in Melbourne. These days it is sometimes still used to refer to a lovable rogue.

Gordon Bennett

A blasphemous oath now regarded as on a par with 'jolly hockey sticks' or 'oopsy daisy', the expression was inspired by the infamous American playboy and newspaper man James Gordon-Bennett who, during the late nineteenth and early twentieth centuries, became widely known for his extravagant lifestyle and shocking behaviour. He once arrived late and drunk at a party in the mansion of the family of his fiancée, socialite Caroline May, and urinated into a fireplace in full view of his hosts until the fire was barely smouldering. The engagement was broken off immediately and Bennett had to flee to France for a while. He also liked to announce his arrival in restaurants by yanking the tablecloths from all the tables he passed. He would then hand the manager a wad of cash with which to compensate his victims for their lost meals and spattered attire. Hence his maligned name lives in the pejorative but amusing cry, 'Gordon Bennett!'

Birkenhead Drill

A British troop ship, HMS *Birkenhead*, hit a reef and sank off Cape Town in 1852. There were only three lifeboats, so the captain gave the order, 'Women and children first!' – the first time this procedure, known as the Birkenhead drill, was used. The ship sank in under 20 minutes, leading to the deaths of around 400 people. Most of those who died were British soldiers and the majority of them were eaten by sharks, as the few survivors later testified, which is why South Africans often refer to Great White sharks as 'Tommy sharks'.

Eddie Would Go

The local saying in Hawaii that 'Eddie would go' refers to Ryon Makuahanai Aikau. Known as Eddie, he was a lifeguard and surfer on the island of Oahu, where he became famous for braving waves of six metres or more to perform a rescue in near-impossible situations. No one lost their life while he served as lifeguard at Waimea Bay. True to his fearless character, while on board a stranded Polynesian sailing canoe in 1978, Eddie decided to venture out on his surfboard in an attempt to find help. Although the canoe with its remaining crew members was eventually rescued, Eddie was never found.

To Fight Like Kilkenny Cats

This means to fight to the bitter end until both sides are utterly destroyed. During the Irish rebellion of 1798, Kilkenny was garrisoned by Hessian soldiers, who entertained themselves by making cats fight each other by tying their tails together and throwing them over a clothes line. Once, as an officer approached to see what the commotion was about, a soldier cut the cats down by their tails. When asked to explain himself, he said that the cats had eaten each other right down to their bloody tails.

Run the Gauntlet

This came into use during the Thirty Years War (1618–48), the word 'gauntlet' being derived from the Swedish 'gatlopp', which means 'lane course' and refers to the narrow passage between two files of soldiers through which another soldier, as punishment, would have to run. The two rows of soldiers (or sailors) facing each other would be handed rope ends to deal out heavy blows to whomever had to run between them.

A brave man is seldom hurt in the back. (Bosnian)

Be brave, not ferocious. (Latin)

Bravery without foresight is like a blind horse. (Iran)

Fear and courage are brothers. (British)

When Greek Meets Greek

This is an expression which indicates that two men or armies of undoubted and indomitable spirit are meeting in a true clash of the Titans and that the contest will surely be severe. The phrase is a reference to the sterling resistance of the Greek cities to the conquests of Philip of Macedon and later his son, Alexander the Great, in the fourth century BC.

Like Billy-O

Meaning to do something with absolute gusto, this phrase probably comes from one of Garibaldi's lieutenants, Nino Biglio, who, during the wars of Italian independence in the nineteenth century, would charge into battle, fearlessly screaming, 'I am Biglio. Follow me, you rascals, and fight like Biglio.'

Saved by the bell

A fun if frightening notion of the origin of this phrase comes from seventeenth-century England when there was a spate of people accidentally buried alive. This seems to be connected with falling unconscious for up to two days after drinking copious amounts of whisky. To avoid hoarsely screaming from the coffin with what one imagines would be the worst hangover in your life, people were buried with their wrists connected to a bell above ground so they could ring it if they became conscious in the coffin. Someone would be on the graveyard shift to listen out for a 'dead ringer'.

Feather in One's Cap

This signifies an achievement or honour and comes from the Native American custom of adding a feather to headgear for every enemy slain. Many cultures had this custom, including Hungary, where at one time a feather was only merited if you killed a Turk.

Cultural Concepts of Bravery

Asatru

This was the name given to Viking beliefs, their pantheon of war-like gods and their belief in Valhalla, the heaven for warriors. Viking chieftains would please their war-gods by their bravery in order to earn a burial at sea, which may have included a ship, treasure, weapons, tools, clothing and even slaves and women buried alive with the dead chieftain.

Omertà

Omertà is the code of honourable silence observed by mafia members but it can also refer to the notion of a society of favours, where people look after and look out for one another. Sometimes people would rather die than disappoint those around them. It comes from the Italian *umiltà*, meaning humility.

Stiff Upper Lip

A concept behind the stoicism of the British Empire, this phrase dates back to the nineteenth century and indicates the correct way to face misfortune and to suppress the display of any emotion.

Buffalo

In Vietnam, fighting buffalo has been a tradition closely connected with the north-coast inhabitants for generations. Everyone, from the elderly to the very young, see the animals as an integral part of life, as they symbolise the people's physical and spiritual strength.

Eagle Feathers

For the Sioux tribe, eagle feathers were the mark of bravery, and they had to be earned. Bravery was a matter of individual freedom; one had to choose to do the right thing. Training began young – babies were not allowed to cry, as the noise could give away the location of the people in a tight situation. Famously, at the Battle of the Little Bighorn, the Sioux cried out: 'Today is a good day to die!' They did not believe death was the worst thing to be afraid of.

Artel

This is an idea from the former communist Soviet Union, and one that embodies the Western concept of team spirit. It involved everyone sacrificing themselves as individuals for the greater good of the whole collective team or the country – one of the core principles in the former Soviet Union – and artels, like army brigades, were set up in workplaces and schools. Their modern-day climbers have used this philosophy to great effect.

Machismo

This puffed-up peacock image from the Spanish and Portuguese has comes to mean male pride, but orginally referred specifically to male chauvinism, which is still acceptable and even expected in some cultures.

Bushido

The Japanese 'way of the warrior' is similar to the concept of chivalry and stresses frugality, loyalty, martial-arts mastery and honour until death.

Quotes about Bravery

Courage is reckoned the greatest of all virtues; because, unless a man has that virtue, he has no security for preserving any other.

SAMUEL JOHNSON
(eighteenth-century English critic)

True bravery is shown by performing without witness what one might be capable of doing before all the world.

FRANCOIS DE LA ROCHEFOUCAULD
(seventeenth-century French author)

The courage of life is often a less dramatic spectacle than the courage of a final moment; but it is no less a magnificent mixture of triumph and tragedy.

JOHN F KENNEDY
(former US president, assassinated in 1963)

Bravery never goes out of fashion.

WILLIAM MAKEPEACE THACKERY
(nineteenth-century English writer)

It is curious that physical courage should be so common in the world and moral courage so rare.

MARK TWAIN
(nineteenth-century US author)

Sometimes even to live is an act of courage.

LUCIUS ANNAEUS SENECA
(Roman philosopher, statesman and dramatist)

A coward is incapable of exhibiting love; it is the prerogative of the brave.

MAHATMA GANDHI
(Indian pacifist, assassinated in 1948)

The French courage proceeds from vanity – the German from phlegm – the Turkish from fanaticism and opium – the Spanish from pride – the English from coolness – the Dutch from obstinacy – the Russian from insensibility – but the Italian from anger.

LORD BYRON
(eighteenth-century English poet)

Bravery is the capacity to perform properly even when scared half to death.

OMAR BRADLEY
(US Army general and commander of US ground forces during the Normandy invasion of the Second World War)

The bravest are surely those who have the clearest vision of what is before them, glory and danger alike, and yet notwithstanding, go out to meet it.

THUCYDIDES
(Ancient Greek historian and author)

A to Z of Bravery

Achilles: the foremost Greek hero of the Trojan War and main protagonist of Homer's *Iliad*.

Arthur, King: the wise king of Camelot in the English Arthurian legend.

Bajazet: fierce, reckless and indomitable sultan of Turkey in the fourteenth century.

Black agate: a gem that makes athletes brave and invincible.

Cid, El: Spanish knight renowned for his exploits against the Moors in the eleventh century.

Crockett, Davy: US folk hero famed as a sharpshooter, hunter and fighter. He was killed at the Alamo in 1836.

David: a boy in the Biblical Old Testament who famously used a sling shot to slay the giant Goliath.

Dunkirk spirit: comes from the notorious Second World War retreat of the Allies from the beaches of France and means to rise to the occasion when confronted by crisis.

Eric the Eel: nickname of Eric Moussambani, the foolhardy, brave but terrible swimmer from Equatorial Guinea who entered the 100-metre freestyle in the 2000 Sydney Olympics and finished last by a huge distance.

Elysium: in Greek mythology this was the paradisiacal land of the blessed, where noble warriors would go when they died.

Filibuster: eighteenth-century bands of pirates who plundered the waters of the Caribbean.

Four-minute mile: the legendary time barrier for running the mile, broken by Englishman Roger Bannister in 1954.

Gepanzerte Faust ('Mailed fist'): a German expression meaning aggressive military might used by Wilhelm II of Germany.

Gurkhas: highly trained and dedicated Nepalese soldiers that have served the British government since the nineteenth century.

Heracles (or Hercules to the Romans): the legendary strong man and son of Zeus from Greek mythology who completed twelve tasks requiring brute strength and ingenuity.

Hillary, Edmund Sir: New Zealand mountaineer who, with Sherpa Tenzing Norgay, was the first to reach the summit of Mount Everest in 1953.

Iron Cross: German medal awarded for outstanding bravery in wartime.

Ivan the Terrible: sixteenth-century Russian tsar who was as brave as he was terrible. He set the foundations for the Russian Empire.

Jackal, the: nickname of the notorious Venezuelan-born hitman and terrorist Illich Ramirez Sanchez, also known as Carlos, who was a hero to the Palestinians but was captured, tried and jailed for life in 1997.

Joan of Arc, St: fifteenth-century peasant leader of the French during the Hundred Years War who was burned at the stake as a religious heretic.

Kublai Khan: grandson of Genghis Khan who expanded the Mongol Empire to include China in the thirteenth century.

Kwuan Ti: second-century Chinese warrior who was raised to be the god of war after his execution. His effigy is kept in most Chinese homes to ward off evil.

Lawrence of Arabia: twentieth-century British crusader T E Lawrence, who became an enigmatic and unprecedented hero in the politics and wars of the Arabs.

Leonidas: Granite-like Spartan king who defeated thousands of Persians at Thermopylae (480 BC) with a few hundred men.

Mandela, Nelson: emerged from years of incarceration as a political prisoner in South Africa to lead his country and end apartheid in the late twentieth century.

Medal of Honor: highest US military decoration for wartime gallantry.

Nebuchadnezzar: greatest king of Babylon (sixth century BC) who restored his country to its former glory and built the Hanging Gardens of Babylon.

Noblesse oblige: French phrase pertaining to the obligation of honourable principles and responsibilities for those of noble birth to help those less fortunate.

Obama, Barack: the first black president of America, inaugurated in 2009.

Ogier the Dane: one of the great heroes of medieval Romance literature.

Pimpernel, Scarlet, the: fictional English aristocrat who risked life and limb to save his French counterparts during the French Revolution.

Prometheus: rebel titan in ancient Greek mythology who stole divine fire from Zeus for man's sake.

Q ships: warships camouflaged as steamers to lure U-boats to destruction in the First World War.

Queensberry rules: a set of honourable rules governing a fair boxing match, formulated in the late nineteenth century and publicly endorsed by the ninth Marquess of Queensberry.

Richard the Lion-Heart: Richard I of England, the warrior king renowned for his prowess in the Third Crusades.

Rob Roy: Rob Roy MacGregor was a highland rogue and folk hero in eighteenth-century Scotland. He supported James II and was regarded as the Scottish Robin Hood.

Saladin: Kurdish Muslim who became the Sultan of Egypt and Syria and led Muslims in the twelfth-century crusades. A great leader in battle who even Christian chroniclers remembered for his chivalry.

Snell, Hannah: the first female marine; in 1746 Snell disguised herself as a man to become a footsoldier and then a sailor in order to look for her husband, who had abandoned her.

Tchaikovsky, Pyotr Ilyich: Russian composer who wrote the 1812 Overture to commemorate the Battle of Borodino, in which Russian forces held off Napoleon's army, breaking the back of the French invasion.

Tsvangirai, Morgan: peaceful leader of the Movement for Democratic Change (MDC) in Zimbabwe presently challenging the brutal rule of President Mugabe.

Ulysses: Roman name for the mythical Greek king of Ithaca and star of Homer's *Iliad* and *Odyssey*. Ulysses came up with the idea for the wooden horse that led to the capture of Troy.

Unknown Warrior, the: an unidentified soldier who was killed in the First World War and brought home from a battlefield on the Western Front to be buried with the kings at Westminster Abbey as a symbol of all the unknown dead.

Verloren hoop: Dutch phrase meaning 'lost troop' that has been adapted into English as 'forlorn hope'. It refers to the body of men selected for a desperate enterprise or mission. Historically, it was often volunteers who were sent to the front to attack.

Victoria Cross: highest British military award for valour.

Wallace, William: thirteenth-century Scottish peasant who led a rebellion again the English and defeated them at Stirling Bridge before he was later hanged, drawn and quartered.

Wehrmacht: name given to the unified armed forces of Germany from 1921 to 1945, responsible for terrible Nazi war crimes but also many extraordinary military feats.

Xavier, Francis: pioneering sixteenth-century Spanish missionary who worked among the poor in India, Mozambique and Indonesia.

Xerxes: Ancient Persian king who was so controlling he even had the sea lashed when it washed away a bridge he had had built.

Yellow jersey: in sporting terms there are few honours as prestigious as receiving the *maillot jaune* in the cycle race, the Tour de France, which is worn each day in the arduous three-week race by the overall leader.

York, Sergeant Alvin: American hero of the First World War who captured hundreds of Germans and won the Medal of Honor.

Zinoviev letter, the: a letter allegedly signed by Russian communist leader Zinoviev in 1924 inciting English communists to rise up, but which was intercepted by MI6 and is now thought to have been a forgery sent as a Red scare by White Russians.

Zorro: the black-masked swordsman and vigilante of old California was the invention of Johnston McCulley in 1919.

7 | Sport

Outrageously Audacious World Football XI

Goalkeeper: Lev Yashin (Russia)
The Black Spider always seemed to have eight arms to stop shots. He saved 150 penalty kicks for the USSR in the 1950s and 1960s.

Right back: Lilian Thuram (France)
Stalwart of the 1998 French World Cup-winning side and the most capped player in French football.

Centre back: Bobby Moore (England)
The definitive tackler and World Cup-winning captain from 1966.

Centre back: Franz Beckenbauer (Germany, captain)
Der Kaiser, as he was known, invented the role of the defensive sweeper and was World Cup-winning captain in 1974.

Left back: Paolo Maldini (Italy)
The Italian has played through the last three decades; perhaps the most perfect defender to have played the game, with great skill, vision and time on the ball.

Right midfield: Garrincha (Brazil)
The diminutive winger was perhaps the greatest dribbler of all time and wowed crowds in the 1950s and 1960s with almost childlike trickery.

Centre midfield: Alfredo di Stéfano (Argentine-Spanish)
The attacking midfielder in this side played internationally for Spain, Columbia and Argentina and, after joining Real Madrid in 1953, he scored a magnificent 216 goals for them.

Centre midfield:	**Lothar Matthäus** (German)
	The engine room of this team. This dynamic midfielder led Germany to World Cup victory in 1990.
Left midfield:	**Johan Cruyff** (Holland)
	The sublime skills of this ambidextrously footed maestro bag him a place on the left, where he can roam to devastating effect. Won European Footballer of the Year three times in the 1970s.
Forward:	**Pelé** (Brazil)
	The legendary number 10 takes his place up front.
Forward:	**Diego Maradona** (Argentina)
	Controversial left-footed player whose awe-inspiring skill was never in doubt. Led Argentina to World Cup victory in 1986.
Subs:	**Bert Trautmann** (Germany, inspiring keeper), **Roberto Carlos** (Brazilian fullback who could strike a thunderbolt with his left foot), **John Charles** (physical but gentle Welshman equally adept as striker or in defence; played at Juventus in the 1960s with amazing goal-scoring record), **Michel Platini** (sublime French passer of the ball from the 1980s), **George Best** (Northern Ireland, the mischievous Manchester United player often had the ball stuck to his feet), **Giuseppe Meazza** (although he would sleep in a brothel the night before a game, he was a great Italian goal scorer in the 1930s for Inter Milan).

Pelé

The Brazilian footballer Pelé is probably the most famous sportsman of all time. His skill on the pitch was sublime and his audacious trickery shone through at a time when huge defenders tried to dominate the game of football with brutal physicality. Every Pelé fan has a favourite moment from this legendary player's repertoire, whether it is a long-range shot, bicycle kick, cheeky header, mesmerising dribble or an outrageous dummy. Recent generations who are growing up with a love for the game should gorge themselves on Pelé video clips.

Edson Arantes do Nascimento was born on 23 October 1940 in Três Coracões, Brazil. The son of a minor-league soccer player, he grew up in an extremely poor neighbourhood, where one of the only sources of entertainment was to play soccer barefoot with any kind of makeshift ball, including bundles of tights and socks. Many players on the Brazilian pitches gained diminutive nicknames – his father was called 'Dondinho' and young Edson took the name 'Pelé'.

Pelé was coached by his father and had a mentor in former soccer star Waldemar de Brito. By the tender age of 11 he had played for his first team, that of the town of Bauru, Brazil, and at 15 he moved to Santos to play professionally for the Santos Futebol Clube. Pelé, also dubbed rather piratically 'the Black Pearl', scored 1,281 FIFA-approved goals in 1,363 games and was arguably the world's most popular athlete.

In 1958 Pelé was selected to go with the Brazilian team to the World Cup in Sweden. He helped his country win its first title, scoring two goals in a dramatic 5–2 win over Sweden in the final. He returned to play for Santos and they went on to win six Brazilian titles. In 1962 he was again part of the Brazilian team that won the World Cup, although an injury forced him to sit out the contest.

In 1970 Pelé played for Brazil's World Cup team in Mexico City. The competition was a magical festival of football with a Brazilian team inspired by Pelé and which also included such greats as Rivelino, Jairzinho and Tostão. Dazzling play, such as his famous 'dummy' which fooled the Uruguayan keeper in the semi-final and his brilliant header in the final against Italy, meant that nobody would forget Pelé's last World Cup.

Trench Football

From the most famous player, we turn to the most famous game of football ever played.

During the Christmas Day truce of 1914 in the middle of the First World War battlefield, the guns fell silent and British and German soldiers left their trenches to play football against each other in the freezing mud of no-man's-land.

Firing ceased along the entire 800 kilometres of the Western front, where close to half a million men were encamped. The truce began on a frosty moonlit Christmas Eve when the Germans began to place lights along the edge of their trenches and venture over to the British trenches to wish them a Happy Christmas.

Then, on Christmas Day, the Germans emerged from their trenches and sang 'Stille Nacht, Heilige Nach' ('Silent Night, Holy Night'), while the British responded with hearty renditions of 'O Come All Ye Faithful' and 'While Shepherds Watched Their Flocks'. In one sector, the British helped the

Pelé stats

He became the most prolific striker in Brazil's history, scoring 77 goals in 92 matches for his country.

Pelé scored 12 goals in three different World Cup tournaments, a record beaten only by Ronaldo.

He is considered by FIFA to be the most prolific scorer in football history, with 1281 goals in 1363 matches in all competitions.

He is the only player to have won three World Cups, although he did not receive a medal for the one in 1962, since he was injured in the second match.

He is one of the few players who have scored in two different World Cup finals; only Paul Breitner, Vava and Zinedine Zidane have also achieved this.

Germans bury one of their snipers and, in another, the Germans produced a Christmas tree and staged the football match. They played an informal game, kicking around empty bully-beef cans and using their caps or steel helmets as goalposts. No official score was recorded.

After the game the troops exchanged autographs, cigarettes and tunic buttons and wished each other a happy new year. In some areas, the truce lasted only one day; in others it continued until close to the new year. Both sets of military commanders forbade it ever happening again. The last known survivor of the Western Front Christmas truce, Alfred Anderson of Angus, Scotland, died in 2005 aged 109.

Legs of Steel

Steve Prefontaine

Running has seen few greater enigmas than this American middle- and long-distance runner. He was born in 1951 and was, as he himself said, 'just a boy from Coos Bay, Oregon' who knew how to win, despite having one leg longer than the other.

He soon discovered his gift for running at Marshfield High School by being aggressive, going out hard and then clinging to the lead – a tactic that his fans and fellow competitors grew to adore and admire. He said, 'No one will ever win a 5,000-metre by running an easy two miles. Not against me.'

He quickly grew from home-town hero to record-setting university phenomenon at Oregon, to internationally renowned track star. He gained national attention and appeared on the cover of *Sports Illustrated* at the age of 19. He developed his hunger to be the best in his field and to do it with style – to show people something they had never seen before. He wanted to excite people and he usually did. As he said, 'Some people create with words, or with music, or with a brush and paints. I like to make something beautiful when I run. I like to make people stop and say, "I've never seen anyone run like that before." It's more than just a race, it's a style. It's doing something better than anyone else. It's being creative.' And he proved himself time and time again. Nobody in the US could compete with his relentless pace.

One of his most glorious failures came during the 1972 Olympic Games in Munich, when he was 21, which was two years younger than anyone else in the 5,000-metre race. In true 'Pre' fashion he grabbed the race by the horns and set the pace for most of it. Perfectly positioned at the bell, he looked poised to burst away at the final corner but simply could not hold his speed. He ultimately finished fourth behind Lasse Viren of Finland, Mohammed Gammoudi of Tunisia and Ian Stewart of Great Britain, who passed Prefontaine less than ten metres from the finish line. He said, 'If I lose, forcing the pace all the way, well, at least I can live with myself.'

To give anything less than your best is to sacrifice the Gift.

On 30 May 1975, returning from a party, Prefontaine swerved his MGB convertible to avoid crashing into an oncoming car, which forced him to hit a rock wall. His car overturned and trapped Prefontaine underneath it, crushing him to death. He was just 24. For a distance runner, Pre had yet to reach his prime, but remarkably he held US records in every race from the 2,000 to the 10,000 metres, as well as the two-, three- and six-mile races. He had even run a mile in 3:54, an excellent time for a distance runner. In one four-way track meet in Eugene in 1973, he ran a 3:56 mile and, incredibly, followed it up with a 13:06 3-mile an hour later.

Prefontaine liked to say, 'To give anything less than your best is to sacrifice the Gift.' He is honoured every year at the Prefontaine Memorial Run, a challenging 10,000-metre road race across one of his old training courses, with its finish line at the high-school track where he first competed.

Faster on One

The Australian sportsman Michael Milton lost his leg to bone cancer at the age of nine but has still enjoyed a glittering skiing career. At the age of 14, Milton competed in the 1988 Winter Paralympics in Austria and in 1992 in France he picked up a gold medal in the slalom, which was the first winter Olympic gold for Australia. He also won the silver medal in the super giant slalom, which incorporates both downhill and super slalom racing. From there on, he achieved a podium place in every event he competed in at every Winter Paralympics. He has won eleven Paralympics medals (six gold, three silver and two bronze). His appearance at the 2006 Winter Paralympics was his fifth and final, after which he focused more fully on the dangerous pastime of speed skiing. In April 2005 he made an astounding daredevil breakthrough by becoming the first person with a disability to break the 200-kilometre mark with a speed of 210.4 kilometres per hour. He then aimed to beat the Australian open record of 212.26 kilometres per hour, set in 1997 by Nick Kirshner and on 19 April, 2006 he became the fastest Australian speed skier after setting a world record of 213.65 kilometres per hour in France.

Milton is now pursuing a new sport: cycling. After six months of intense training, he not only won a gold medal in the 3,000-metre pursuit at the Australian Track Cycling

Championships in February 2007, but also broke the Australian record.

His dream to make the Australian team and compete at the 2007 Para-cycling World Championships were sidelined when he was diagnosed with oesophageal cancer in July 2007. He has since made an amazing comeback from this serious illness, recording times at the 2008 Australian Track Cycling Championships comparable to his results in the same event 12 months before.

Hours and Fells

Fell running, which is running and racing off-road and always involves steep inclines, is a sport full of granite-like competitors in the UK and is based in the rugged peaks of the Lake District. One of the stars of the sport, 'Iron'

When it's really hurting, go faster and then the hurting will be over sooner.

Joss Naylor, ran through every kind of discomfort, from a tongue so swollen he could barely drink, to finishing with both feet cut through to the nerve. He held every record in the sport and, 12 years after having two discs removed from his back, he ran up 72 peaks in 24 hours in 1975 to extend the Lakeland record, which is the blue-riband challenge of the fells.

The original barrier which led to the record and is still seen as the benchmark for top fell runners is the 'Bob Graham Round'. This challenge is similar to breaking the four-minute mile or climbing Mount Everest. It involves a 72-mile course over 42 Lake District peaks with 8,230 metres of ascent and descent which runners aim to complete in under 24 hours, thus matching Graham's achievement in 1932. The Bob Graham 24-hour club now has close to 1,000 members and is still a glorious badge of honour.

Carlos Sastre: A Profile of the Cleanest Tour de France Winner

Who? Quirky, introspective 33-year-old Spaniard who has been in the top ten of the Grand Tours for nearly a decade and hails from the hill town of El Barraco, north of Madrid.

When? The Spaniard pulled off a tremendous performance in the 2008 Tour.

How? Always in contention for the Yellow Jersey, he attacked at the bottom of the Alpe d'Huez and somehow managed to put two minutes between himself and his closest rivals with the bravest ride of his career. He then rode an impressive time trial to hold off his main rival, Cadel Evans.

Surprise winner? People knew he could climb but he had never previously time-trialled well.

Attacking rider? A popular misconception is that Sastre is a follower and never attacks. But he attacked to chase Floyd Landis in 2006 and again in 2007 to try to bring back Alberto Contador.

Fell running has a long history. There have always been races in the hills between nimble shepherds as part of community fairs and games, such as the Burnsall Feast Sports in West Yorkshire, which is still going today.

The modern incarnation of the shepherd is IT project manager Mark Hartell from Cheshire, who broke the Lakeland record in 1997 by running up an extraordinary 77 peaks in 24 hours. It is no surprise that his philosophy is: 'When it's really hurting, go faster and then the hurting will be over sooner.'

In his prime, Hartell was an amateur who must have been one of the most extraordinary all-round athletes in the world. He is a world master of endurance races, claiming, 'I've always been better over long distances, though it is difficult to keep going at six miles an hour for a very long time.'

Hartell started fell running in his twenties, after orienteering and climbing, and completed the Bob Graham Round when he was 27. He has now cemented his place in fell-running folklore by breaking the Lakeland 24-hour record in 1997. 'I broke it on my third attempt, which makes it more meaningful. My best moment was descending Grisedale Pike – the final peak of 77, knowing I would complete [my dream] within 24 hours, after years of visualising about that moment.'

Hartell's other achievements include: the Scottish 'Ramsay Round' solo; joint winner with Mark McDermott of the Hardrock 100 run in Colorado; the Grand Slam of ultra-running in the US (four 100-mile trail races); and the record time for the Welsh 'Paddy Buckley Round' – 18 hours, 10 minutes.

His versatility has stretched to the most hostile environments on earth. He has been the highest-placed Briton in the Marathon des Sables in Morocco, which is a 160-mile ultra-marathon across the Sahara Desert, in which he finished thirteenth in 2002. In the same year, he came fourth in the Everest marathon.

Hartell says, 'When I am running I think of how lucky I am to be there – in other words I am privileged to be able to have the time, money and physical ability to be taking part. I also have the certain knowledge (from experience) that pain is temporary but defeat is permanent.'

Ultimate teamwork

A Russian climbing dream team have managed some of the toughest climbs and the most daring freefall exploits. Having grown up under a communist regime and almost bred to endure, their leader, Alexander Odintsov, provides a fascinating insight into how far climbers will go for adventure.

In 2004, he and his team climbed the seemingly impossible north face of Jannu, a mountain in the Himalayas. Most of them were seriously injured in the attempt but they still managed to cling to the face of the mountain for months to reach the summit.

Here is an extract from an interview with Odintsov recorded by Italian journalist Vinicio Stefanello:

> In 30 years 25 teams from all over the world attempted to climb the direct line up the north face of Jannu: none succeeded. And you can be sure that they were amongst the best climbers in the world. Our main objective was to climb the mountain. To achieve this we had to choose the best style of ascent, bearing in mind the level of mountaineering worldwide and the objective.

Clean rider? Sastre has tested clean while many others were testing positive for performance-enhancing drugs and his team CSC led the way with their anti-doping programme. Sastre said, 'I know I'm clean. I know how much I suffer and how much I have given for this.'

Masterplan? Sastre peaked at the right time. Cadel Evans had raced more that year and therefore wasn't as fresh by the end.

Style? Mountain climber. Hunched over with the now-familiar smiling grimace. A canny rider who sometimes sandbags.

Inspiration? Sastre almost retired in 2004 after he broke his elbow and a year after his brother-in-law, the mythical climbing legend José Maria 'El Chaba' Jiménez died from cocaine poisoning. Sastre said in tribute, 'I believe he was there with me on the line. His spirit is with me all the time. He's the person I learned most from in life and about cycling.'

Character? From the school of eccentric climbers, Sastre is almost horizontally laid-back and spiritual about his sport. Very much the family man.

>>>

Career? Sastre began his career as a *domestique* for the ONCE team. He moved over to Bjarne Riis' CSC team in 2002 and became team leader after Ivan Basso was involved in a drugs scandal. Sastre was third in 2006 and fourth in 2007.

Lucky year? Yes, the previous year's winner Alberto Contador was not there because of a ban on the Astana team but Sastre made his own luck and has been unlucky himself that the sport has not always been so clean. He has now joined the new Cervelo team as their team leader.

It was indescribably terrible. Only three out of our ten mountaineers didn't get injured – seven had problems. It was a war. Had we been armed with five people, had our army been too small, then we would have lost before reaching the last section of the climb, the steepest. Had we attempted the face in alpine style then we would have had to live at 6,500 metres for a month. In our situation, in the society of world climbers, all can understand that this was impossible. There were only two options: either we had to have extremely strong team members, stronger than normal climbers, or we had to move quickly. There is no human being that combines these two factors. There is no human being who can live above 7,000 metres for such an extended period of time, on a wall such as Jannu and with those difficulties. It is not humanly possible.

We planned everything so as to succeed, and right from the start we had envisaged all possible problems, also because we had all the information from everyone who had attempted the Wall before us. We knew everything about the difficulties and the misfortune of the other teams that had preceded us. Every attempt had a reason for failure. On the basis of this analysis and these experiences, we chose the best way to approach and resolve this problem.

None of us are young; we all grew up in the Soviet era. We're used to working as a team and the prime objective of the team is to reach this objective. Man slips into second place. What you want is of secondary importance.

When you understand that freedom cannot exist, then this in itself is a certain type of freedom. If you understand that freedom is not eternal, that freedom cannot be timeless, that your personal freedom can be removed, then you become more free than before. Don't you think that the freest people are criminals? Because they have all forms of freedom, they can even go and kill someone ...

So the concept is: to reach the objective, everyone decides to lose some personal freedom, because reaching this objective gives greater freedom to all.

There was no joy at all when we reached the summit. Because where we suffered most was during the descent from the summit.

The north face of Jannu was a dream for all, for many generations of mountaineers, for the best in the world. This means that we too realised this dream. And what happens to people who realise their dreams? They are unhappy. What should they do next? All mountaineers are ready to suffer hardship, regardless of their nationality. The difference between the Russians and the rest of the world is that we are organised better.

Dangerous Rides

Palio di Siena

One of the most traditional and dangerous horse races in the world is the Palio, a maniacal 80-second bareback horse race, held twice a year in the city of Siena, Italy, in July and August. It has been run for over 350 years.

Seats around the town square are sold out months before. The three-lap race circles the Piazza del Campo in the city centre. The outer course is covered with a thick layer of dirt and the corners are protected with padded crash barriers. There are 17 city wards, or *contrade*, each represented by a horse, but only ten mounts are permitted in each race. In the second race the seven that haven't yet taken part compete, together with horses from the first, drawn by lots.

The dardevil jockeys on nine of the horses enter the course and jostle for position between two ropes. The race starts when the tenth horse, the *rincorsa*, is allowed to enter, releasing the front rope. The beginning is so crucial and can take a long time, as often deals have been made between the *contrada* and the jockeys to ensure a better start. The race has a long history of bribery, corruption and doping. And then they're off!

It's a crazy course. On the dangerous, steeply canted track, the riders are allowed to use their whips (in Italian, *nerbi* – stretched, dried bulls' penises) not only for their own horse, but also for disturbing other horses and riders. As a result there are some spectacular falls, but it's a pulsing, vibrant scene as the crowd wave their handkerchiefs in the colours of their *contrada*, colours which are also worn by the horses dashing round the piazza. The winner is the first horse to cross the finish line with its head ornaments intact – and a horse can win without its rider (known as *cavallo scosso*). The loser in the race is considered to be the *contrada* whose horse comes second, not last. The winner is awarded the Palio, a banner of painted silk.

There may be some danger to spectators from the sheer number of people in attendance and it can, on occasions, be brutal – in the Palio held on 16 August 2004 the horse for the *contrada* of the *Bruco* (Caterpillar) fell, was badly trampled and died of its injuries.

Yak racing

Ninety-five per cent of the world's population of yaks live on the Tibetan plateau and are an integral part of day-to-day life:

they transport people and cargo; warm clothes are made from their wool; their milk and meat provide food; and their dung is used for fuel. But they can also run, and surprisingly fast, especially in sprints. On the Tibetan plateau, in Qinghai and Mongolia, yak races are an essential local pastime.

The races are usually arranged as side events to other activities, such as horse races, and are an indispensable part of traditional festivals. Every yak is decorated elaborately with red tassels on their heads, silk on their horns, ornamented saddles, ribbons on their ears and fan-shaped Tibetan patterns on their tails.

Originally there were 50 or 60 yaks in each race but now there can be as many as 150 trying to run the 2,000 metres. It takes great strength and skill to remain on the yak when it is galloping. In horse-racing, skill and speed usually determine the winner, but in yak-racing, luck also plays an important part. Yaks have not been domesticated and tend to be highly undisciplined beasts. Their unpredictability adds to the excitement of the spectacle. Many races have ended at places other than the finish line, since a yak may decide to stop and eat or go off in a completely different direction. The animals may shoulder and fight each other, or may jump and give a backward kick mid race. They have also been known to charge the audience. Such events make the Grand National seem like a pony trek.

This stop–start crazed race/rodeo takes the yak and its rider close to eight minutes to complete. The winner becomes famous locally and enjoys special treatment from his master. The rider is usually given several *khata* (a traditional Tibetan scarf) as well as a small amount of prize money. Yak-racing is also performed in parts of Kazakhstan, Kyrgyzstan and Pakistan.

Ten Sportsmen and -women Who Played through the Pain

These feats of extreme bravery are just as often regarded as utter stupidity, but there is nothing more a fan appreciates than a player who can show their true mettle in these situations.

Bert Trautmann

The German goalkeeper earned his place in football folklore when he played on for 15 minutes after breaking his neck in Manchester City's 1956 FA Cup final against Birmingham. The team won that day and Trautmann continued playing for many years after his injury.

Tyler Hamilton

The American broke his collarbone in a spectacular crash in the 2003 Tour de France but carried on cycling for two weeks in the endurance race, finishing fourth overall and somehow managing to pull out a stunning performance to win stage 16.

Malcolm Marshall

In 1984 in a test match against England at Headingley, West Indies bowler Malcolm Marshall broke his thumb; however, not only did he produce a match-winning bowling spell but he also batted with one hand and scored a boundary.

Shirley Muldowney

Muldowney was the first woman to race and win at the highest levels of professional drag-racing in the US. In 1984 she crashed at nearly 400 kilometres per hour and spent 18 months recovering from the injuries to her legs. She insisted the surgeons set the bones in her shattered right foot to insure that she would be able to press the accelerator and as a result she returned to race – and win – for several more years.

Valeri Zelepukin

The Russian ice-hockey player went out to play for the New Jersey Devils in the National Hockey League with an agonising cruciate-ligament tear. Just when everyone thought he could no longer keep playing, he went off, put on a knee brace and rejoined the match.

Mohammed Ali

In 1973 Ali had his jaw broken by Ken Norton in round two of their heavyweight fight but still managed to fight another ten rounds. He narrowly lost the bout in the end but a surgeon later said he had no idea how Ali had fought with his jaw bones more than half a centimetre apart.

Niki Lauda

When Lauda's Ferrari burst into flames at Nurburgring at the 1976 German Grand Prix, the Austrian was later given his last rites. But within six weeks he was back in a car at Monza. He finished fourth and ultimately lost the drivers' title by a point, but drove with his healing burns still bleeding through his balaclava.

Wayne Shelford

This All-Black number eight had metaphorical balls of steels. In a match against France in 1986, Shelford suddenly had his scrotum ripped apart by a French boot. Unperturbed by the sight of one of his testicles hanging out, nonchalantly moved to the side of the pitch, where the physio stitched him up. Shelford returned to the fray and played on.

Abebe Bikila

The barefoot-running Ethiopian won two Olympic marathons, one of them, in Tokyo, only six weeks after surgery for acute appendicitis. He then had a car crash that tragically left him paralysed from the waist down. Two years later he had recovered enough to win a 25-kilometre cross-country sledge race in Norway even though he had never before experienced snow conditions.

Cal Ripken Junior

The Baltimore Orioles baseball player was riddled with injuries throughout his career, during which he nevertheless played an astonishing 2,632 consecutive Major League games. His most serious injury was a herniated disc, which prevented him from sitting down. He could also barely walk, but an anti-inflammatory he took later meant that he somehow was able to take to the pitch, despite being in excruciating pain.

The Last of the Great Matadors

Spaniard José Tomás is a throwback to a bygone era, a mythical *torero* amid the mediocrity of modern matadors, many of whom had started behaving like spoilt footballers – at least according to the Spanish press.

Born in Galapagar, near Madrid, Tomás, now 33, was always destined to be a different kind of bullfighter. This son of a village mayor faced his first bull at the age of 14 and launched his career in Mexico. Wiry and forlorn with a melancholic countenance, Tomás is an unconventional and introspective recluse who shuns media attention and is often compared to Cervantes' Don Quixote.

He has never honoured the bullfighters' tradition of praying to the Virgin Mary, nor did he dedicate the bulls he killed in front of King Juan Carlos to the monarch, and he has even broke bullfighting's greatest taboo on two occasions by not killing the bull: once when he believed the bull had not been up to scratch and once when he felt he had not performed well himself.

His quiet, upright and tranquil style has been compared by many to the great Manolete, who died after being gored by a bull in 1947. Tomás's mesmerising grace draws huge crowds from all over Spain. He walks slowly across the ring as if in a mystic trance, remaining motionless as the bull approaches and rarely moving back a pace with each death-defying feint. He was once heard to say, 'When I go to the bullfight, I leave my body in the hotel.'

Tomás makes a point of refusing to show fear, an attitude that has led to his being gored about 20 times during more than 400 bullfights. He is seen as having recaptured the sense of danger that modern bullfighting was losing, attracting fans from all over Catalonia, where the popularity of the sport had been on the wane.

The risky confrontation between a powerful beast and a vulnerable human being remains the essence of the sport and it was Tomás who revived this.

A Great Comeback

There is no sport more visceral and unforgiving than boxing. There is no tougher arena than that ring into which two men climb, going toe to toe with one another until both are barely able to breathe or stand.

Of all the golden periods of boxing, few can match the light-middleweight, middleweight and welterweight divisions at the start of the 1980s, which contained a crop of brilliant boxers, including Panamanian Roberto Durán and the Americans Thomas Hearns, Sugar Ray Leonard and Marvin Hagler.

Sugar Ray Leonard v Marvin Hagler

In November 1982, the welterweight and middleweight champion, Sugar Ray Leonard, announced his retirement from boxing. He had just had his eye surgically repaired following a great title fight he had narrowly won by knockout (KO) against Thomas Hearns. Leonard said a bout with Hagler would unfortunately never happen.

He later decided to make a comeback but had to delay it for more corrective surgery on his eye. Eventually he returned against Philadelphia's Kevin Howard in February 1984 and was knocked flat on his back for the first time. At the post-fight press conference, Leonard surprised everyone by announcing his retirement again, saying he just didn't have it any more.

But in May 1986, Leonard announced he would return to the ring for one more fight against world middleweight champion Marvin Hagler, a phenomenal opponent. Many believed Leonard would lose as he had been so inactive and his eye injuries had worsened. Hagler took a few months to decide, then agreed to the match, which was scheduled for 6 April 1987 at Caesars Palace, Las Vegas.

The bout was promoted as 'The Superfight'. In exchange for more money, an over-confident Hagler agreed to a 12-round limit (which guaranteed WBC sanction) and a big ring. But he was still the favourite, with the odds starting at 4–1, then settling at 3–1. Leonard had fought once in five years, and had never fought as a middleweight. But it was only Hagler's third fight in two and a half years.

The fight was a quintessential clash of styles: Hagler's blue-collar and bull-like aggression against the smooth-talking con man Sugar Ray, who looked to make his sting.

What was not realised at the time was the lengths Leonard had gone to prepare for the fight. He had painstakingly trained himself and was in great shape. It later transpired that he had fought several 12-round bouts behind closed doors and, as a result, was more battled-hardened than anyone knew.

Hagler started cautiously, falling behind on all cards. Leonard used the same tactics that he had used in his famous 1980 rematch against Roberto Durán: speedy lateral movement and jabs and clinching when he was in trouble. Hagler had trouble keeping up with Leonard's fancy footwork and found himself chasing shadows round the ring. Leonard frustrated the champion by avoiding toe-to-toe exchanges – which he could not win – and by scoring points with weak-arm punches.

The bout finally came alive in round nine. As a vexed Hagler surged forwards like a wounded bull in search of the knockout punch, Leonard used all of his guile and durability to stay on his feet. Hagler landed the harder blows but the laser-like hands of Leonard kept on with the flashier flurries. They were so rapidly fired that they were almost like cartoon-character combinations. But although Hagler later claimed they did not hurt him, the jabs had been connecting. The two boxers fought right up to the final bell to a roaring crowd. No one quite knew who had won.

It was one of the great fights of all time. Neither fighter had been knocked down. Leonard had been warned repeatedly for holding by the referee, but no points were deducted. Hagler had landed the bigger punches but Leonard the showier ones. The decision went to Leonard via a split decision. Some critics claimed that Leonard's Las Vegas-style showmanship had deceived the judges into awarding him a false victory; others claimed his brilliance had just shaded the fight. Hagler bitterly protested the result and, utterly disillusioned, never fought again. Leonard fought on, clashing with Hearns and Durán again before quitting for good after a 1997 loss to Hector Camacho. Boxing fans and writers still argue over the decision of the Hagler fight.

The Roundabout

1980 Durán bt Leonard

1980 Leonard bt Durán

1981 Leonard bt Hearns

1983 Hagler bt Durán

1984 Hearns bt Durán

1985 Hagler bt Hearns

1987 Leonard bt Hagler

1989 Leonard v Hearns (draw)

1989 Leonard bt Durán

Great Moments of Bravery

One of the smallest players in world rugby is one of the best. In 2008 the dazzlingly talented Welshman Shane Williams won the IRB International Player of the Year award for his sizzling performances on the Welsh wing. His style of play has always excited the crowd whenever he gets the ball. He can turn on a sixpence, has a deceptive sidestep and his acceleration off the mark is incredible. The French, who know magical talent when they see it, call him Peter Pan.

Evidence of his fleet-footed agility abounds but possibly none greater than the try he scored in the second test against world champions South Africa in the summer of 2008. When a ball suddenly squirted out of the scrum on the blind side, Williams was the first to scoop it up. With six South African defenders covering, he made a lightning-quick burst down the wing into the space ahead.

'I thought I'd turn inside first, see if I could find some support,' Williams explained. 'But nobody was there, so I thought maybe I could turn them outside and go for the corner. It all happened so perfectly: as soon as I turned one way, the defender's head turned the opposite way and I thought, "I've got a chance here", so I just pinned my ears back and went for it. It happened in a split second but it felt like an eternity. I still chuckle about that one.'

The bemused Springbok captain, John Smit, who was one of the defenders who failed to get a finger near Williams, was astonished by his mercurial run. 'He's a freak of nature – I don't know anyone else who could do that.'

Five Courageous Female Firsts

First to Swim the English Channel

On 6 August 1926, the 19-year-old American Gertrude Ederle became the first woman to swim the 34 kilometres across the English Channel. She did it in 14 hours and 31 minutes – nearly 2 hours faster than any man had at that time.

First to Play on the Men's Golf Tour

The multi-talented athlete Babe Zaharias, who had also been a basketball and baseball player, competed in the Los Angeles Open in January 1938, a men's PGA event, a feat no woman would try again till 60 years later. The American missed the cut on this occasion but afterwards went on to make the cut in every PGA tour event she entered.

First to Run a Sub-Three-Hour Marathon

On 31 August 1971, Adrienne Beames of Australia became the first woman to run a sub-three-hour marathon with a remarkable time of 2:46:30.

First to Ever Score Points in Formula One

The Italian racing driver Lella Lombardi participated in 17 Grand Prix. She scored a total of 0.5 championship points, and is the only female Formula One driver in history to have a top-six finish in a world championship race, at the 1975 Spanish Grand Prix. Half points were awarded for this race due to a shortened race distance.

First to Pole Vault Over Five Metres

The 27-year-old Russian athlete Yelena Isinbaeva is already a two-time Olympic gold medallist (2004 and 2008) and world sportswoman of the year. On 22 July 2005, she became the first female pole vaulter to clear five metres, a height many men cannot clear. She has broken the world record 28 times. And counting.

8 | Escape

Five Famous Prison Breaks

Tower of London, United Kingdom

In 1716, William Maxwell, Earl of Nithsdale, who had been incarcerated during the first Jacobite rising, escaped from the Tower with the help of his brave young wife, Lady Nithsdale. She brought him a disguise of women's clothing on the eve of his execution and helped him sneak out in a lady's cloak. The Nithsdales then escaped to Rome in the disguise of servants to the Venetian ambassador. They lived together in Rome for over 30 years.

Doge's Palace, Venice, Italy

In 1756, Italian writer Giacomo Casanova fashioned a spike out of a metal bar and made a hole in the roof of his cell with the help of the prisoner in the adjacent cell, a priest called Father Balbi. They then managed to climb out onto the roof and, with the help of ropes and ladders, lower themselves into a room below. They changed their clothes and waited until early the next morning when they broke a lock and scurried through corridors, galleries and chambers to an outside door. Ultimately, they escaped via gondola from one of the most secure prisons of the time.

Alcatraz, United States

This tiny island off the coast of San Francisco was famously impossible to escape from. But in 1962, with a few spoons, a homemade raft and shedloads of ingenuity, Frank Lee Morris and brothers Clarence and John Anglin made it off the island. They placed dummy heads made of soap, toilet paper and real hair in their beds to fool prison officers checking on them at night. Meanwhile, they had cut through the back of their cells with sharpened spoons, and found a ventilation duct to crawl through. Their raft was a few pieces of driftwood tied together. None of the escapees have been heard of since and no bodies have ever been found.

Klong Prem Central Prison, Thailand

In 1996, Briton David McMillan managed to escape from Thailand's hard-line Klong Prem Central Prison while awaiting trial on drug charges. With the threat of the death penalty hanging over him, McMillan cut the bars of his shared cell with a hacksaw, and negotiated four walls before scaling the prison's electrified outer perimeter using a bamboo ladder. He then skirted the moat while hiding his face under an umbrella from the prison factory. Within four hours he had managed to board a flight to Singapore with a fake passport.

Grasse High Security Prison, France

Pascal Payet was initially sentenced to a 30-year jail term for a murder committed during the robbery of a security van. Following two previous jailbreaks, Payet escaped from Grasse prison in 2007, using a helicopter that had been hijacked by four masked men from Cannes-Mandelieu airport. The helicopter picked him up on the prison roof and landed some time later at Brignoles on the Mediterranean coast. Payet and his accomplices then fled the scene and the pilot was released unharmed. Payet was recaptured just over two months later, in Mataró, Spain. He had undergone cosmetic surgery but was still identified by Spanish police.

Papillon

The autobiography of French convict Henri Charrière is one of
the greatest ever tales of escapology and the indomitable
nature of the human spirit. Though some of its authenticity
has since been questioned by historians, it is always worth
telling nonetheless.

Arrest and Sentencing

Born in 1908, 'Papillon', as he was called due to the butterfly
tattoo on his chest, escapes from a life in the French Navy by
amputating his thumb. He moves to Paris and becomes known
and respected in the criminal underworld. In 1931 he is
arrested for the murder of a pimp, a crime he denies, and is
sentenced to life imprisonment in the French penal colony of
Guiana.

The Voyage

On the cramped convict boat heading for South America
many prisoners carry their own 'chargers' – slim metal
cylinders inserted into the nether regions, where money is
stored in order to make a break. Papillon keeps his high in his
intestine. He makes a wealthy friend in Louis Dega, a high-
rolling fraudster whom he promises to protect and who he
knows might be able to help him finance an escape.

First Breakout

On 29 November 1933, just after he arrives, Papillon feigns
illness with two friends, Clousiot and Maturette, and is
transferred to hospital. Maturette entices the guard inside the
ward with the offer of sex but instead clubs him over the head.
All three escape to the jungle and make their way to a leper
colony on Pigeon Island, where the fine manners of Papillon

stand them in good stead. The lepers equip them with a boat and supplies. Papillon is moved to tears by their kindness. Soon the three convicts are away on the high seas in a tiny vessel sailing along the coast via Trinidad and Curacao to Riohacha, Colombia.

They are joined by three additional escapees but poor weather prevents them from leaving the Colombian coast and they are all recaptured and imprisoned. Papillon saws through his bars and manages to escape with a Colombian called Antonio who, after feeding him with coca leaves for several days and nights to keep him awake, helps them both get miles away. Then they separate and Papillon braves the territory of the feared Indians of the Guajira. He finds a coastal village and not only is he accepted by the natives but he takes two sisters as wives and lives in the earthly paradise, where he fishes for pearls and makes love under the stars. But he becomes restless. Though he may later regret leaving such a life, he presses on, desperate to return to France and seek vengeance against those who wronged him.

Colombian Black Hole

Before he can return, Papillon is betrayed by an Irish nun and incarcerated in a fetid hole at Santa Marta. His basement cell is pitch-black and sporadically floods with filthy water, rats, centipedes, crabs and black sludge. He emerges 28 days later half-blind and covered in scabrous bites.

Barranquilla

After Santa Marta he is moved to the prison at Barranquilla, where he is reunited with Clousiot and Maturette and makes five unsuccessful escape attempts:

1. The prisoners try to escape *en masse* from the chapel during the Sunday service, some armed with knives and revolvers. The warders foil the attempt and three prisoners are shot in the process.

2. He tries to drug the guard's coffee with a sleeping draught so he can climb over the wall unnoticed, but the potion takes too long to work and a new guard comes along, thus foiling any hope of escape.

3. He cuts the bars of his cell with a hacksaw but makes the wrong jump from the roof in the dark and falls over 15 metres, breaking heel bones in both feet. He is caught and beaten by the guards and is left flat-footed for the rest of his life.

4. He eats a large dose of crystallised picric acid until he is yellower than a lemon to try to get to a hospital and escape from there. But he is such a security risk they only let him go to the sickbay under armed guard for a couple of hours.

5. After smuggling in dynamite by paying the guards, Papillon lights a fuse to blow up a prison wall. The huge explosion wakes the whole neighbourhood but does not create a hole big enough to escape through.

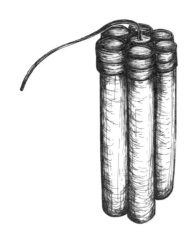

First Solitary

Believing that he is a beaten man, Papillon is eventually extradited back to French Guiana. As punishment he is sentenced to two years' solitary confinement on Saint Joseph Island, 11 kilometres off the coast of French Guiana. Clousiot and Maturette are given equal sentences. Kept in almost total darkness in a punishment block known as the 'man-eater', the prisoners must observe strict silence and survive on watery soup and stale bread for the length of their confinement. Papillon observes: 'The Chinese discovered the drop of water that falls on your head. The French discovered silence.' His friends sneak in a coconut a day to keep him strong and Papillon disciplines himself. He walks back and forth all day in his three-by-three metre cell and daydreams for hours at a time.

Murder
Clousiot is released and dies soon after and Papillon is transferred to Royal Island. His next escape plan, which is to secretly build a raft, is foiled by an informant, Bébert Celier, whom Papillon then stabs to death for his treachery.

Second Solitary
Papillon receives a death sentence in all but name: eight more years of solitary confinement. Psychologically, the first year almost drives away his will to live, but on one of the few occasions when he is taken outside, the daughter of one of the wardens falls into shark-infested water. Papillon risks his life by jumping into the sea and saves her. He is granted a reprieve and is allowed out of his cell after 19 months.

Insanity
French Guianese officials decide to support the pro-Nazi Vichy regime, which means the penalty for any escape becomes capital punishment. This throws a spanner in the ongoing machinations of Papillon, who quickly realises he must act insane to make any progress, reasoning that insane prisoners cannot be sentenced to death and that the asylum is less heavily guarded. He collaborates with another prisoner, but this escape attempt fails. As they sail away, their boat is destroyed against the rocks. The other prisoner drowns and Papillon is nearly dashed to death himself.

Sweet Taste of Freedom

Papillon returns to the regular prisoner population after being 'cured' of his mental illness. He is now sent to Devil's Island, from which no one considers breaking out: the prisoners instead spend their time gambling and gardening. No one can believe that Papillon is willing to risk the dungeons again but he goes out on a limb. He finally succeeds by throwing himself off a cliff attached to a bag of coconuts and lands on a freak wave, which he has calculated will take him out to sea.

Accompanied by a friend called Sylvain on another bunch of coconuts, they drift for days in the burning sun, living off coconut pulp. When they reach the mainland, Sylvain forgets that the shore is mostly swamp and slowly sinks into the mud and dies while Papillon desperately tries to get to him.

From there he makes contact with another escapee – a Chinese man called Cuic Cuic who's hiding out on an island in the swamps with the aid of a cunning trick. He owns a pig that always finds a sure path across the shifting ground. Cuic Cuic is so attached to the pig that, when they make their break on a new boat, the pig comes with them. Papillon eventually ends up in Venezuela, where, after some time in jail, he's given an identity card and, phew, gains his ultimate freedom.

Leading to the Promised Land

Moses of the Railroad

Harriet Tubman was a great liberator and a woman for whom action always spoke louder than words. She grew up in Maryland and was wounded badly in the head by a slave owner. As a result, she suffered from disabling fits and headaches for the rest her life. But such suffering seemed only to galvanise her resolve. Unlike many women born into slavery she seized her own road to freedom in 1849 and then helped countless others escape through the Underground Railroad, a network of secret routes and safe houses.

Tubman was so effective that she had a price on her head and was often referred to as Moses. Regardless, she continued to travel to the South and lead out small bands of fugitives who were sheltered by contacts she had picked up en route over the years. Her steely determination and true grit meant she never gave up on those in her care. If one of them, exhausted, refused to go and wanted to turn back, she would point her revolver at them and say, 'Go on or die.'

Later, she nursed soldiers during the Civil War and became a heroine for the Union cause: she became a scout and a spy and reported on enemy troop movements. In June 1863 she accompanied Colonel James Montgomery, who commanded the black regiment at Port Royal, on a gunboat raid in South Carolina. They raided and burned Confederate plantations and freed 750 slaves. An article in the *Boston Commonwealth* newspaper, 10 July, read, 'Col. Montgomery, and his gallant band of black soldiers, under the guidance of a black woman, dashed into the enemy's country, struck a bold and effective blow and brought off near 800 slaves. Many times she has penetrated the enemy's lines and discovered their situation and their condition, and escaped without injury, but not without extreme hazard.'

Tubman was a strong woman who loved her family, her people and her nation and was happy to risk her life countless times for the sake of emancipation and the abolition of slavery.

She eventually moved to Auburn, New York, where she died of pneumonia at 73 years old. Her words are inscribed on a tablet placed in her memory at the entrance to the Auburn courthouse: 'I nebber run my train off de track an' I nebber los' a passenger.'

Dull Knife

Dull Knife, the Cheyenne chief, and his band of followers were brought down from the Black Hills of Dakota to an Indian reservation in 1876. The warmer climate was too harsh for them and many started to die from malaria. The Indian leaders appealed to the American people and some were permitted to return to their land; however, proud Dull Knife's band of Cheyennes were not successful in their plea.

The authorities regarded him as dangerous due to his prowess on the battlefield and his indomitable will. As more of his people died he decided to take matters into his own hands and lead them back to their northern hills. This was a very dangerous mission: they would have to escape from the American army all through Kansas and Nebraska. Dull Knife somehow managed to evade all pursuing troops and reach the promised land – their land. But, after their arrival, his people, who were now worn down and weary, were surrounded and taken to Fort Robinson. They decided to make one last stand. Dull Knife said, 'I have lived my life. I am ready. If our women are willing to die with us, who is there to say no?'

They fought until their ammunition ran out, then stuck their chests out as targets, with the women even holding up their babies to be shot.

Although the Cheyenne suffered a heavy defeat, with many dying heartbroken, Dull Knife managed to escape again by sneaking through enemy lines; however, he was obliged to live the rest of his life on a reservation with the few other surviving Cheyenne at Rosebud Valley. He died in 1883. He left a great legacy for his people – inspiring them to continue fighting for their land and freedom.

Great Escapes in War-time

Colditz Disguise

In 1942 Airey Neave became the first British soldier to escape from Colditz, the infamous German prisoner-of-war camp, which Nazi propaganda had proudly proclaimed to be 'escape-proof' and where all troublesome POWs were kept. It was a schoolboy tale of derring-do in which the Eton- and Oxford-educated officer – who had already been mentioned in dispatches and awarded the Military Cross for bravery on the battlefield – teamed up with Dutch officer Tony Luteyn to stage an escape so outrageous that if it weren't true you wouldn't dare to believe it.

On 5 January 1942, after the evening roll call, Neave and Luteyn were led to the castle theatre by 'escape officers', Briton Pat Reid and Canadian Hank Wardle. Both were dressed in three sets of clothes: civilian clothes underneath, then German uniform and their own uniform on top. Through a hole under the theatre they were led inside a tower, where they could reach the stairs to the guardroom. The two escapees waited a few minutes to allow Reid and Wardle time to return to the theatre and camouflage all traces of their route.

Neave and Luteyn then stripped off their own outer uniform and cleaned and checked their German kit before proceeding downstairs. They wandered into the castle guardroom with their noses in the air. Then, with Luteyn chatting in fluent

German, they casually sauntered past the guards and ordered them to stand to attention – which is why, one assumes, no one had a chance to question their cardboard badges. Several guards even sprang to attention when 'Lieutenants' Luteyn and Neave passed by.

But their journey was far from over. They quickly scuttled to the park because passing the final gate required identification, which they didn't have. Fortunately it was only lightly guarded and they clambered up and over the wall without a hitch. They buried their German uniforms and went to Leisnig where they took the early train to Leipzig.

This was a real test for their already frayed nerves. In Leipzig they had to wait a nail-chewing 12 hours before they could continue to Regensburg and so decided to pass the time by going to the cinema. They finally reached their next destination of Ulm through Regensburg and Augsburg, where they tried to buy a ticket to Engen, a village near the border town of Singen. But the woman selling train tickets smelled escaped Allied rats and warned the police. The men were rounded up, taken to the local police station and questioned. There they told their cover story: that they were Dutchmen working for the Arbeitseinsatz (enforced work detail). The police only half believed their tale and took them to the local Arbeitseinsatz building to check their story.

Here, as was becoming only too customary, they escaped again and walked 40 kilometres to Biberach, where they caught a train to Stockach. In the freezing cold they then travelled for four days on to Singen, living on a few morsels of chocolate and sucking snow to ease their burning throats. On the third night they slept on a park bench and found their shoes frozen to the ground when they woke. They managed, between bouts of tears and laughter, to defrost them with their breath. As they approached the Swiss border on the fourth day, they picked up tools in the hope of looking like local workers.

The border was being patrolled by a police car and there was no way through; however, this was the final hurdle to freedom and they both knew they had to risk it. They decided to shake hands, wish each other luck and make their own separate runs.

Both of them were suffering from bleeding blisters on their feet, but their mad dashes through the deep snow were successful, and they happily reached the Swiss village of Ramsen. From there they made their way through neutral Switzerland and then through Vichy France to Spain, Gibraltar and safety, in one of the most cherished feats of British pluck and deadpan Dutch resolve.

After their glorious escape, Luteyn went to Suriname (a Dutch colony at that time) and then to Australia to join the remainder of the Dutch East Indies Army. For his part in the escape Luteyn was awarded the Bronze Cross in 1943. Neave continued to live life in the fast lane, working as an intelligence agent for MI9, and later he went on to become a famous Conservative politician who masterminded Margaret Thatcher's rise to power. He was killed in an IRA car bomb in 1979, possibly due to his links to the intelligence services in Northern Ireland.

In the freezing cold they then travelled for four days on to Singen, living on a few morsels of chocolate and sucking snow to ease their burning throats.

MI9

This little-known sub-section of British Military Intelligence was set up by ex-infantry major Norman Crockatt in 1940 to support resistance fighters and help men escape and avoid capture at all costs. It became a very successful organisation

and not only assisted in countless escapes but gave troops hope that escape might be possible and therefore lifted morale for many prisoners of war. Half a million Britons were trained in evasion and escape techniques during the Second World War.

MI9 devised various escape aids to send to POW camps. There were compasses hidden inside pens or tunic buttons which used left-hand threads, so that, if the Germans discovered them and the searcher tried to unscrew them open, would just tighten. There were maps printed on silk, and disguised as handkerchiefs. For aircrew there were special boots with detachable leggings, so that they could be quickly converted to look like civilian shoes and the hollow heels contained packets of dried food.

MI9 then set about cunning ways to hide these escape aids. They placed tools inside cricket bats, put blades inside combs, and arranged maps and forged German identity cards in the backs of books and inside gramophone records. There were even board games that concealed money. MI9 sent the tools in parcels and in canned goods in the name of spurious charity organisations, though in time the German guards learned to intercept much of the escape booty.

MI9 was able to build up lines of helpers who were prepared to risk their lives to shelter fugitives on their way out of occupied territory. These lines worked very well in Belgium and France, though not so well in the Far East, where Caucasians stood out. A grand total of more than 33,000 men from British, American and British Commonwealth forces made their way back to the Allied lines either as escapees or

evaders, after being inside enemy territory. Many of them were assisted, sometimes unbeknown to themselves, by MI9 or its American equivalent, MIS-X.

Escape to Death

As the moon shone on the POW camp in Cowra, Australia, on 18 August 1944, the Aussie guards manning their sentry towers had little idea of what was about to happen. The camp was full of Italians captured by the Allies in the Middle East and Japanese who had been fighting on the islands just north of Australia.

The Italians saw no lasting disgrace in surrender and accepted it as a necessary part of the fortunes of war. They were content to see out the war as prisoners on foreign soil; however, the Japanese found the act of surrender to be deeply humiliating. Many adopted false names when they were captured so that their brothers-in-arms and families would presume them dead.

The Australian guards were aware of these strongly held beliefs but were confident there would not be an outbreak: any attempt at escape would be suicidal, and was therefore unlikely. The prisoners had no real weapons and no means to obtain arms. Furthermore, any attempted escape would involve negotiating the three barbed-wire perimeter fences and metres of entangled barbed wire that lay between them. The camp perimeter was dominated by six guard towers, each about nine metres high, and was regularly patrolled by armed guards. Then there was the small matter of escaping from a huge and dusty continent which, of course, was once a giant penal colony.

When a bugle rang out at 2 a.m. on that August night, all hell broke loose. The POW huts were set alight and cheers of 'Banzai!' rang around the camp as a thousand Japanese suddenly charged the fences just like the Charge of the Light Brigade – and with equal chance of success. They brandished filed-down cutlery and baseball bats and had only baseball mitts and blankets to protect them from the barbed wire.

Almost immediately the first waves were mown down by machine-gun fire from the Australian guards, but these sentries were soon overwhelmed by the sheer weight of numbers and killed. The Japanese just kept on coming, treading over the bodies of their fallen comrades and scaling the barbed wire. The next three waves of escapees broke through the fences, crossed the perimeter wire and escaped to freedom. So far dozens had been killed and nearly 100 wounded just to get out.

The POW huts were set alight and cheers of 'Banzai!' rang around the camp ...

But their freedom was short-lived. Though 330 were on the loose their Asian features made them conspicuous and they were on a giant dusty continent with nowhere to run to. They were rounded up after 10 days a mere 50 kilometres away. Many escapees chose to take their own lives in an act of harakiri rather than be recaptured. Two threw themselves under an oncoming train, while many hanged themselves. On their recapture, some pleaded to be shot and few surrendered peacefully. At least two prisoners were shot by local civilians and several by military personnel. During the breakout, 231 Japanese and four Australians died. The Japanese self-imposed order that no civilians were to be harmed was obeyed. It was one of the bravest yet most foolish breakouts in history. The Australian prime minister, John Curtin, later described the actions of the POWs as showing 'a suicidal disregard for life'. But to the Japanese it was the true honour of the code of *bushido* (see also Samurai, p. 81).

Escape from Death

Slovakians Alfred Wetzler and Rudolf Vrba were two of a very small number of Jews known to have escaped from the Auschwitz death camp during the Holocaust. It was one of the most valuable escapes in history; not only did they save their own lives but they also saved the lives of thousands of Hungarian Jews.

In the early afternoon of Friday, 7 April 1944, with the help of men in the camp's Polish underground movement at Auschwitz, the two men got through the barbed-wire inner perimeter and clambered into a hollow dugout in a woodpile that had been assembled to build huts for the new arrivals.

Nevertheless, the dugout was still inside an external perimeter fence. The other prisoners placed boards around the hollowed-out area to hide the men, then sprinkled pungent Russian tobacco soaked in gasoline around it to fool the guards' dogs. The two remained in hiding for four nights barely allowing themselves to breathe for fear of being caught by the Nazis and executed immediately.

Finally they sneaked out from the woodpile wearing Dutch suits, overcoats and boots they had taken from the camp, and escaped through a hole under the external perimeter fence. They made their way south, walking parallel to the Sola river, heading for the Polish border with Slovakia 133 kilometres away, guiding themselves using a page torn from a child's atlas that Vrba had found in the warehouse.

After their successful escape they both compiled a priceless 32-page document, known as the Vrba–Wetzler report, using

Top Ten Must-See Escape Movies

1. *Le Grand Illusion* (1937)
Considered one of the greatest French films of all time, Jean Renoir's masterpiece is regarded as the classic prison-break movie.

2. *The Colditz Story* (1955)
A classic yarn starring John Mills, about Allied prisoners planning numerous escapes from the 'escape-proof' German POW camp housed in a castle.

3. *A Man Escaped* (1956)
This is a well-observed, minimalist film based on the memoirs of French Resistance activist André Devigny, who was imprisoned by the Nazis and condemned to death. But he devoted all his hours to planning an elaborate escape.

4. *The Great Escape* (1963)
This popular film deals with the true story of the largest Allied escape attempt from a German POW camp during the Second World War. It chronicles the process of secretly digging three tunnels (called Tom, Dick and Harry) and the prisoners' valiant attempts to escape before they are either captured or shot.

evidence they had smuggled out of the camp with them. It explained the horrifying inner workings of the Auschwitz camp with details of the gas chambers, crematoriums and, most convincingly, a label from a canister of Zyklon gas. The report was the first detailed report about Auschwitz to reach the West that the Allies regarded as credible. The evidence eventually led to the bombing of several government buildings in Hungary, killing Nazi officials who were instrumental in the railway deportations of Jews to Auschwitz. The deportations halted, saving the lives of up to 120,000 Hungarian Jews.

Escape from the Jungle

Lieutenant Dieter Dengler was a German-born pilot in the US Navy who was shot down by anti-aircraft fire during the Vietnam War. He managed to crash-land his Skyraider in Laos, and when his squadron mates heard the news, they remained confident he would be rescued. Dengler had a reputation as a maverick and a renegade. The ops officer was always after him to get a haircut and Dengler was forever in trouble over his uniform or lack of military manner. In his German accent, he would protest with a wry grin, 'I don't understand.' But he also had a great reputation from the Navy survival school where he had escaped from mock-POW camps three times.

However, the day after his landing he was captured by Pathet Lao communist guerrillas. They bound his hands and marched him through the jungle, stopping at various villages along the way. At one point he escaped and climbed a tower in the hope of signalling a passing aircraft. But lack of shelter from the sun and his thirst forced him to climb down to seek water, and his captors found him as he was drinking from a spring. They began to torture him without mercy. They dangled him upside down, slathered him with honey and put ant nests on his face until he passed out. They suspended him in a freezing well at night so he couldn't sleep and inserted bamboo shoots under his fingernails and skin. He was also kicked, battered with rifle butts and dragged behind water buffalo. They also made a rope tourniquet around his upper arm, inserted a piece of wood, and twisted and twisted until his nerves were cut against the bone. His hand was completely unusable for six months.

Dengler was eventually taken to a prison camp near the village of Par Kung, where he met other POWs, including Duane Martin, a US Air Force helicopter pilot who had also been shot down, Thai civilians Pisidhi Indradat, Prasit Promsuwan and Prasit Thanee, YC To, who was Chinese, and another American, Eugene DeBruin. They had all worked for Air America.

They had been in the hands of Pathet Lao troops for over two and a half years when Dengler joined them. The day he arrived in the camp and saw the state of the other prisoners (one had pus all over his teeth and another was carrying his own intestines) Dengler immediately advised them that he intended to escape and take them with him. They were surviving off just a single handful of rice to share while the guards would stalk deer, pulling the grass out of the animal's stomach for the prisoners to eat while they shared the meat. The only 'treats' were snakes they occasionally caught from the communal latrine, or the rats that lived under their hut, which they could spear with sharpened bamboo.

Nights were worse. The men were handcuffed together and shackled to medieval-style foot blocks. They suffered chronic dysentery, and were made to lie in their excrement until morning.

5. *Midnight Express* (1978)
Based on a true story, Billy Hayes is caught attempting to smuggle hashish out of Turkey. The Turkish courts decide to make an example of him, sentencing him to more than 30 years in prison. Hayes is very badly treated in a Turkish prison and ends up in a mental asylum. Eventually he runs out of patience with the appeals made by his lawyer and the US government and he escapes to Greece after killing the prison warden.

6. *Escape from Alcatraz* (1979)
Clint Eastwood plays inmate Frank Morris, who masterminded the famous break from Alcatraz in 1963.

7. *The Shawshank Redemption* (1994)
Based on a Stephen King novella, the film tells the story of Andy Dufresne, who is sent to Shawshank prison to serve a life term for the murder of his wife. Although he eventually adapts to prison life, he exacts a remarkable revenge on the prison authorities.

>>>

8. *The Count of Monte Cristo* (2002)

The young Edmond Dantès is betrayed by his friends in Napoleonic France and incarcerated as a political prisoner in this rip-roaring adaptation of the Alexandre Dumas novel. Dantès escapes and wreaks his slow revenge with the help of a cache of hidden treasure.

9. *Rescue Dawn* (2006)

Director Werner Herzog's film tells of the real-life story of US fighter pilot Dieter Dengler, the German-American shot down and captured in Laos during the Vietnam War.

10. *The Children of Huang Shi* (2008)

Sixty orphaned Chinese boys attempt a dangerous journey across the Liu Pan Shan mountains into the Mongolian desert to escape the Japanese invasion in 1937. Leading them is a young Englishman named George Hogg, with the help of Chen Hansheng, the leader of a Chinese partisan group.

There was strong debate among the prisoners about escape until one of the Thais heard the guards discussing the possibility of shooting them in the jungle and making it look as if it were an escape attempt. It is also likely they witnessed their captors beheading an American Navy pilot and executing six wounded marines. Everyone then agreed to go.

On 29 June 1966 the prisoners, spurred on and led by Dengler, managed to relase their hands and feet from painful shackles. They made their move and in a mad dash managed to get the weapons from the guards, who were busy eating. Dengler picked up a submachine gun and rifle from the sentry hut, and shot three guards in the resulting melee. Another guard was shot by one of the Thais and they all made it into the jungle, where they had to get as far as they could before help came from the Pathet Lao troops.

Dengler and Martin went off by themselves with the intention of heading for the Mekong river to escape to Thailand. They made their way down a creek on a raft and found a river. They set up camp in an abandoned village, where they found shelter from the nearly incessant rain. They had brought rice with them and berries and a little corn, but were still on the verge of starvation. They managed to light a fire and were convinced they had signalled a C-130 airplane, but no rescue force appeared.

They had been going for 18 days and Martin, who was weak from starvation and suffering from malaria, wanted to approach a nearby Akha village to find food. Dengler, who was suffering from jaundice, knew it was not a good idea, but refused to let his friend go alone. Disaster struck. They were seen by a local child who alerted the village and were soon approached by a man with a machete. Martin and Dengler knelt down in supplication but the villager struck Martin twice, nearly decapitating him. Dengler jumped to his feet and ran screaming at the man, who returned to the village to get help. Dengler then escaped into the jungle, where he successfully hid himself away.

Over 20 days later, in a jungle infested with leeches, insects and parasites which he was now eating to keep himself alive, Dengler managed to signal a US Air Force pilot with a parachute he had found and rocks with which he had written *SOS*. A rescue force was dispatched but the helicopter crew restrained him when he was brought aboard, thinking he could be a Viet Cong.

Dengler said one of the flight crew who was holding him down pulled out a half-eaten snake from underneath Dengler's clothing and was so surprised he nearly fell out of the helicopter. They stripped him to be sure he wasn't armed or in possession of a hand grenade. When questioned, Dengler told them that he had escaped from a North Vietnamese prisoner-of-war camp two months earlier.

It wasn't until after he reached the hospital at Da Nang that Dengler's identity was confirmed. The US Navy flew him to the *Ranger*, his former ship, for a welcoming party. He was the only American flier ever to escape from a POW camp in the impenetrable Laotian jungle. From there he was airlifted back to the US, suffering from malnutrition and parasites.

With the exception of Indradat, who was recaptured and later rescued by Laotian troops, none of the other prisoners were ever seen again. DeBruin was reportedly captured and placed in another camp, then disappeared in 1968.

A Day in the Life of...
Mama Muliri, rape counsellor and rescuer in the eastern region of the Democratic Republic of Congo

6 If you are female in the Congo you are fair game to the many armed militias that roam the forests. Hundreds of thousands of women have been raped during and after a brutal civil war that erupted in 1998. Officially the war is over but the fighting and brutality continues.

Wading into this sea of horror is 'Mama' Muliri, a formidable 40-year-old Congolese woman, a mother and rape counsellor who ventures into the far-flung war-torn jungles to help women escape and bring them to a clinic at the regional capital, Goma, for medical and psychological treatment.

Muliri said, 'Here, today the number of rapes can be down and tomorrow up again, because when there is new fighting there is new rape. The work is very, very hard but the need is so high. I travel far, often on foot. But apart from the physical difficulty I have to listen to so many traumatic stories that it affects me. I put myself in the victim's place and often get depressed.'

She says that most of the victims are attacked by rebel militias, but also by the government soldiers, many of whom are little more than brigands in government uniforms. Frighteningly, the patients are usually aged 11 or 12. The health clinic in Goma is one of only two hospitals in a country the size of Western Europe designed specifically to deal with the medical aftermath of sexual violence.

The impact on the victims is irrelevant to their attackers, nor are the attacks much to do with sexual desire or gratification. Muliri says, 'The real targets are the husbands, brothers and fathers left demoralised, humiliated and emasculated by the rapes.' Most of the patients Mama Muliri brings in suffer from fistula, a tear between the anus and vagina often causing incontinence. Every year more than a thousand women and girls are treated for this at the clinic, at a rate of almost four per day.

Muliri says her latest patient is Marie, who is 13 and tiny with stick legs, wide eyes and short hair pulled into neat cornrows. She was brought in by Mama Muliri from her home near Kindu, an hour's flight to the west (there are no roads through the thick jungle). Muliri had heard about Marie from the network of female informants she has built across the east of the country and had gone to find her.

Marie was carrying bananas from the

market when four armed men stopped her. Two of them snatched the fruit from her and started to eat while the other two dragged Marie off the path, stuffed a banana in her mouth to shut her up and raped her. Then the men swapped and the other two took their turn. They left her bleeding on the ground. Mama Muliri explained that, although Marie's rapists were arrested, they bribed the authorities the equivalent of a few dollars and were released.

Marie has had the surgery to repair her damaged body and is receiving counselling for her damaged mind, but as Mama Muliri then adds, 'How are we supposed to tell her that she has HIV? '

9 | Death

Roman Gladiators

Gladiators were heart
throbs. Graffiti scrawled
over the walls of Rome
proved testament to this:
'Crescens, the net fighter,
holds the hearts of all the
girls and Celadus, the
Thracian, makes all the girls
sigh.' Even the mother of
the Emperor Commodus is
believed to have had a huge
crush on the gladiator
Martianus.

The first gladiators were slaves who were made to fight to the death at the funeral of a distinguished aristocrat, Junius Brutus Pera, in 264 BC: the more human blood spilled at a funeral, the easier the deceased's journey to the underworld.

Though modern tastes may recoil at the concept of watching people die, fighting nobly to the death was at the very heart of the Roman psyche and civilisation. It was part of their culture and no morality questioned it at the time. Over time, gladiatorial spectacle became separated from funeral rites of passage and began to be watched for pleasure. The adversaries continued to be slaves, but free men also volunteered. Even a few emperors fought in the Colosseum. It was the most dangerous 'profession' ever known to man, one that forced its participants to kill or be killed with as much dignity as possible.

For a few it brought great fame, great wealth and the honour of being awarded full freedom and given a *rudius* (special wooden sword) as proof of the achievement. Just as street kids today may rise through the ranks in professional boxing or soccer (with a little less risk of losing a limb or being decapitated), so too could gladiators find glory.

Main Fighting Styles

Various fighting styles evolved from the different types of combat the Romans encountered when they fought and conquered such civilisations as the Thracians, Samnites, Celts and Gauls. Fighting styles became stereotyped to add to the theatre of the occasion and a gladiator might be schooled in a style quite different from the method of his actual place of origin. To provide the audience with extra thrills, the combatants were taught to aim at the major arteries under the arm and behind the knee. Very occasionally there were female gladiators in the arena. The different types of gladiators included:

CATAPHRACTARIUS

The Cataphractarii preferred to bludgeon their way to victory than fight with any finesse. These big, abrasive gladiators were one of the most heavily armed and their style was based on that of the Sarmatians from Central Asia. They fought with a long lance known as a *contus* that was so heavy it had to be wielded with two hands. It could be either an infantry pike or a rider's lance, leaving no free hand to carry a shield.

The Cataphractarii had thick protective helmets and head-to-toe scale armour,similar to chain mail. This weighty, slow-moving gladiator would often have been paired with a lightly armed gladiator who fought in a nimble gladiatorial style, such as the Retiari.

DIMACHAERUS

An ambidexterous gladiator who fought wielding two swords. The swords were short curved scimitars known as *siccae*, with blades around 43 centimetres long. The Dimachaeri were lightly shielded, with leather leg and arm strapping and possibly a tight-fitting helmet. They would have been pitted against a heavily armed gladiator, such as the Murmillo.

EQUITES

The Equites were trained horsemen and fighters. They were armed with a short and light throwing spear, a *gladius* sword (64 centimetres or so in length) and a fair-sized round cavalry shield. They also wore a sleeveless tunic and a *galea* helmet, which would be topped off with ostrich or eagle feathers.

Bustuarii: slave gladiators that fought to the death at funeral ceremonies of prominent Romans.

Essedari: fighters with long spears on chariots reflecting the warfare of the Celts in Great Britain.

Naumachiarii: gladiators who would fight to the death in mock sea battles.

Praegenarii: mock gladiators who fought with blunt weapons to amuse the crowd in intervals.

Provocator: the only gladiator to have a breast plate; fought other Provocatores.

Rudiarius: a gladiator who had won his freedom but still might come back to fight to milk the crowd that idolised him.

Sagittarius: fought with a bow and arrow on horseback as a speciality act such as a battle re-enactment.

The Equites always fought each other. The first round of combat resembled a knight's joust, when they would pass and throw their spears at each other before dismounting and fighting to the death on foot.

GALLUS

This was a heavily armed gladiator based on savage warriors from Gaul (ancient France) that the Romans were accustumed to fighting on the battlefield. Protected with a *galea* helmet, leg armour and leather wrist and arm protection, they also carried a large rectangular *scutum* shield and a *gladius* sword. These gladiators were trained at the Ludus Gallicus, the smallest of the gladiator schools.

HOPLOMACHUS / SAMNITE

Named differently at different times in Roman history, they were more heavily armoured fighters based on the Greek hoplite. They were usually well-built men who were not very agile but could wield hefty weaponry. They would use a *gladius* sword to thrust and parry rather than cut and slice, and they might also carry a dagger called a *pugio* and a lance. For defence they carried a small bronze shield called a *parmula*, wore a *galea* helmet and sported an *ochrea* (metal greave) on one leg. They fought similarly armed gladiators.

RETIARIUS/LAQUERARIUS

Retiarii fought in the rather unusual style of fishermen. The tactics were to tangle an opponent from long range with a net and then skewer him with a trident. This gladiator would also have a small dagger in case he had to get messy in very close combat. He was supposed to be agile, skilful and quick and would fight against a Murmillo emblazoned symbolically as a fish and very heavily armed. Retiarii wore long tunics, had no shield or helmets and therefore no anonymity and were often viewed as evasive and effeminate because of their clothing and tactics. The Laquerarius was very similar to the Retiarius, but used a lasso instead of a net and a lance instead of a trident.

MURMILLO / SECUTOR

These bare-chested bruisers evolved to fight the Retiarii and were supposed to be heavily armed fighting fish. They were armed with the *gladius* sword, the large rectangular *scutum* shield, leather leg and arm protection and a specially designed helmet with a fish design and very narrow eye holes to prevent injury by the trident of the Retiarii.

THRACIAN

A dynamic, lightly armed and popular gladiator, the Thracian fought with the *sica*, a short scimitar, and a small round shield like the one used by hard men from the northern area of Greece on which they were based. They wore a helmet with a tall crested griffin, decorated in feathers and with a visor to protect the face. They also sported leather on their sword arm and a pair of metal greaves to protect their legs. Thracians fought Murmillones and Hoplomachi.

BESTIARIUS / PAEGNIARIUS

These gladiators were specially trained to fight wild beasts in the arena, such as tigers, lions and leopards, using a spear, a knife or a whip (Paegniarii only used a whip). They were popular with the crowd and often the animals were handicapped with bonds on their limbs or semi-caged. These restrictions on the animals made it easier for the gladiator, who would sometimes fight from the relative safety of a spherical round cage. However, the crowd were fickle and would occasionally demand that the animals win.

Scissores: heavily armed gladiators who fought with swords shaped like shearing scissors to produce more bloody effects.

Tertiarius: an understudy to top gladiators who would step in last minute if necessary.

Velites: gladiators armed only with spears; often used in groups to portray large battles.

Famous Gladiators

Flamma

This Syrian was perhaps the all-time crowd favourite. Awarded the *rudius* sword no less than four times, he still chose to remain a gladiator. He lived until 30, fought 34 times, won 21, drew 9 and lost 4 times.

Emperor Commodus (AD 161–92)

Incredibly, this Roman emperor was one of the most famous gladiators, and his appearance in the arena in the film *Gladiator* was more akin to truth than the story of Maximus himself. Commodus regularly took part in the games and spectacles and ordered his fights to be inscribed in the public records and announced in the city newspaper. He called himself the 'Roman Hercules' and fought unhurt 735 times. Basking in the attention and with insatiable bloodlust, he cruelly slew his hapless opponents, whose weapons were as useless as blunt carrots.

Spartacus (c. 109–71 BC)

This famous Roman slave was immortalised by actor Kirk Douglas in the Hollywood film of the same name. He was probably a prisoner of war from Thrace, sold as a slave to a gladiatorial school near Capua. Here he was trained in combat before he sparked a rebellion of slaves to fight the Roman Army. His chief cohorts in arms were two gladiators from Gaul named Crixus and Oenomaus. He failed nobly and his surviving men were crucified.

Priscus and Verus

These two gladiators fought each other for hours to a standstill in the Colosseum and both conceded defeat at the same time. Upon the urging of the crowd, Emperor Titus awarded victory to both of them and presented each man with the *rudius* sword. They both walked from the arena through the Gate of Life as free men.

Marcus Attilus

Attilus was Roman citizen who was in debt and sold himself to a gladiator school for money. He emerged from training to defeat the champion of Emperor Nero, Hilarus, who had won 13 times in a row. Attilus was a natural and triumphed over other gladiators, including Raecius Felix, who had won 12 times in a row before his defeat.

ANDABATA

This sight-restricted gladiator, who wore a helmet like a shrouding hood to limit his vision, was regarded as light entertainment. Andabatae would often be condemned criminals who would fight to the death for a little comic relief in between the main gladiatorial combat. They were armed with a sword and dressed in a loin cloth with no armour or shield and sent out in groups. They would have no idea where to aim their blows and would be goaded and pushed together by arena attendants as they lashed out blindly and wildly, much to the amusement of the mirthful crowds.

The Rite of Death

The actual killing of a gladiator was barbaric but fascinating. It was not over quickly or sloppily, but once it had been decided that the vanquished fighter was to be killed, a ritual took over. The defeated and wounded gladiator would offer his neck to the sword of his conqueror as best he could, trying to take a position on one knee, gripping the other man's leg.

Men were taught how to die at their gladiator schools and their neck would search out the blade when they had their throats cut. It was all part of the performance and the Roman obsession with a graceful death. A gladiator would do his utmost not to scream when he was killed and would never ask for mercy. It was a code of honour and a sure sign that man could lift himself in dignity above beasts.

There was another more grisly show to ensure the corpses were truly dead and to milk any more entertainment out of the ceremony. A Hermes character would enter the arena and prod the corpses with a red-hot iron, while another, dressed as the ferryman of the underworld, Charon, would use a large mallet to smash the skulls of any men who were still alive.

Top Five Efficient Executioners

Twisted bravery this may appear, but executioners who could put people to death quickly and competently, and occasionally painlessly, while avoiding a very sticky mess, were a rare commodity throughout the ages.

1. Albert Pierrepoint

Pierrepoint stood on the shoulders of two other great English executioners: Richard Brandon, who perfected severing a head with a single blow in the seventeenth century, and William Marwood, a Victorian who refined the long drop to kill a man instantly with the noose.

Albert was the last of the Pierrepoint family to serve as Official Executioner of Great Britain and Ireland. He became the most prolific hangman in British history and hanged over 400 people. But he was also the most efficient. The swiftest execution on record took place at Strangeways Prison on 8 May 1951. James Inglis was led from his cell and pronounced dead seven seconds later. Pierrepoint's expertise took him to Germany, where he was responsible for executing around 200 Nazi war criminals after the Nuremberg trials.

2. Charles Henri Sanson

Charles Henri Sanson attracted record numbers to public executions in Paris during the French Revolution. From a lineage of executioners, he was instrumental in the adoption of the guillotine to increase efficiency. He once executed 300 people in three days during the Reign of Terror and was asked to slow down because residents of a nearby street were complaining that the stench of blood would drive house prices down. He was so skilled that he could guillotine twelve people in under three minutes. Marie Antoinette was one of his victims in front of 200,000 cheering fans.

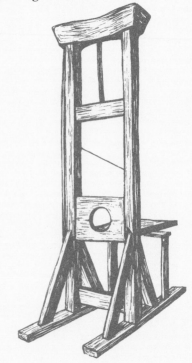

3. Giovanni Battista Bugatti

'Mastro Titta', as he was known (a corruption of 'Master of Justice'), is considered a national hero in Italy for performing 516 public executions for the Papacy. While other executioners on this list would show off for the crowds, Bugatti just got on with it. Although he was necessarily brutal, using hammers to crush heads and then quartering the bodies, he approached each execution in a casually efficient and religious man ner. First he would go to confession and take communion, and then he would offer his victim a pinch of snuff before ending their lives.

4. Souflikar

Mahomet IV's head *bostanci* (executioner) in the Ottoman Empire had a record second to none. He was expected to keep the court in order by strangulation. There was considerable sport involved: the condemned man had to race Souflikar through the gardens to the execution spot. If the man won he was merely banished; if he lost he was strangled to death on the spot. Over five years Souflikar strangled 5,000 victims at a rate of three a day.

5. Grover Cleveland

This American president carried out two executions while serving as sheriff in Buffalo, New York. He hanged a man who'd stabbed his own mother and a few months later he hanged a murderer. During the 1884 elections, Cleveland's rivals called him 'Buffalo's Hangman' which barely affected his candidacy. Some historians believe that because he had personally executed criminals, he was seen to be tough on crime. Modern presidents are unlikely to go to such lengths.

Firefighters

Firemen are going to get killed. When they join the department they face that fact. When a man becomes a fireman his greatest act of bravery has been accomplished. What he does after that is all in the line of work. They were not thinking of getting killed when they went where death lurked. They went there to put the fire out, and got killed. Firefighters do not regard themselves as heroes because they do what the business requires.

Chief Edward F Croker,
Chief of Department, FDNY

September 11: Captain Patrick Brown

'Two hundred and twenty days of boredom, and twenty minutes a year of sheer terror' is how the best friend of Patrick Brown, Captain John Drennan, described firefighting.

Drennan nearly perished with two other men in 1994 when he was fighting a fire inside a building and a gas cloud exploded. But he was resilient and lived for 40 days with fourth-degree burns over most of his body. During this time he was looked after by his best friend Captain Patrick Brown, who wasn't put off his profession by seeing his best friend in so much pain. He was a born firefighter and, as a local bar owner, Steve Schlopak, who knew him well, said, 'When they find Pat Brown, they'll find him in the densest place, in the highest part of the building, with the most firefighters round him.'

He was right. Captain Patrick Brown died performing his job in the World Trade Centre. An ex-marine and Vietnam War hero, Brown then gave 24 years of service to the FDNY, in which time he became one of the department's most decorated men. He always donated any reward to the Burn

Unit at Cornell University Medical Centre. With Brown it was always said he was in the right place at the right time (or the wrong time if you were anyone else) and that when Brown walked down a street a fire would break out and young women would start crying out to him from their windows to be saved.

His final assignment was at the prestigious Ladder 3 Company on East 13th Street in Manhattan. There he developed a reputation for quiet bravery and integrity and firefighters would request transfers to his firehouse to work with him.

On 11 September 2001, Patrick and eleven men from Ladder 3, which is very close to the Twin Towers, were some of the first men on the scene. Along with other rescue workers, they managed to help evacuate over 25,000 people from the burning buildings. It is believed that Brown and his men were on the fortieth floor of the North Tower with around 40 severely burned people when the building collapsed.

The last words of Patrick Brown:

> I'm on the thirty-fifth floor, OK, OK? Just relay to the command post we're trying to get up. There's numerous civilians at all stairwells, numerous burn injuries are coming down. I'm trying to send them down first. Apparently it's above the seventy-fifth floor. I don't know if they got there yet. OK, Three Truck and we are still heading up. OK? Thank you.
>
> — (Captain Patrick J. Brown, tape from 9/11/2001, released on 8/16/2006)

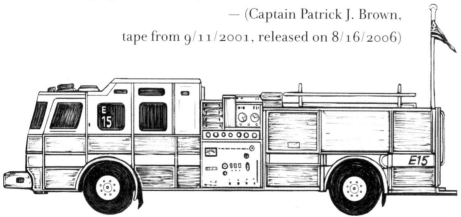

'I am just going outside and may be some time.'

Spoken before his sacrificial walk into a blizzard on Scott's ill-fated Antarctic expedition, Oates was afraid that his lameness would hinder his team's chances of survival.

2. Marie Antoinette, Queen of France (1755–93)

'Pardon me, sir. I did not do it on purpose.'

Spoken after accidentally stepping on the foot of her executioner, Charles Henri Sanson, as she went to the guillotine.

3. Ernesto Che Guevara, Argentinian Revolutionary (1928–67)

'I know you have come to kill me. Shoot, coward, you are only going to kill a man.'

Spoken to his executioner, Mario Terán, a Bolivian soldier.

Chernobyl: Vasily Ignatenko

The reactor leak from the Chernobyl nuclear power station in 1986 is the worst nuclear disaster in history. Design flaws combined with human error caused an explosion at the plant in the former Soviet Union (now Ukraine) that was so powerful it blew off the 1,000-ton cover protecting reactor number four. The ensuing fire raged for 15 days, creating a cloud of radioactive smoke and debris that reached a kilometre into the sky.

Nine tons of radioactive material were released into the atmosphere, almost 90 times the amount released by the Hiroshima bomb. The cumulative death toll will be hundreds of thousands. Almost the whole world has been affected.

'Liquidators' was the loose term given to the 800,000 firemen, divers, helicopter pilots, soldiers, builders and nuclear experts conscripted into the Chernobyl area in the aftermath of the disaster to put out the fires and undertake the immediate recovery work. By all accounts it was an apocalyptic scene, with some of the liquidators living in tents about 200 kilometres from the reactor. Dressed in surgical robes with gloves and masks, they were given shovels to bury the trash heaps, gardens, wildlife, wells, trees and even houses. Their nightmare mission was to bury all contaminated land and property.

This even meant cutting up trees and plants and covering them in plastic sheets before they could be buried. Wildlife was buried dead or alive and altogether the exercise created million of acres of torn-up earth.

But the worst job was the immediate containment on the roof of the ruined reactor. The people who dealt with this were the real heroes. They battled the reactor despite the intense radiation: they put out the fires, they pumped water into the reactor or bathed it in liquid nitrogen and they dropped sand and lead from helicopters. Three divers went down into the pools beneath the reactor to open sluice gates and never came back. Thirty or so men were exposed to such high radiation that they sacrificed their lives within two weeks. But such heroism was necessary to prevent further disaster and to save millions of others.

Among the first firefighters on the scene was one of the resident firemen at the nuclear plant, Vasily Ignatenko, who went in routinely on the night of 26 April to quell the inferno at his workplace. His equally brave wife, Lyudmilla Ignatenko, gave a poignant account in which she demonstrates a dignity and innate loyalty to the people of the Soviet Union in contrast to the insensitive and pragmatic way she has been handled by the Russian authorities. The situation has failed to dampen her sense of humour or her spirit, even though her life has been blown apart by the disaster. Russian journalist Svetlana Alexievich showed nearly as much courage to get such an interview under the suspicious and watchful eyes of the authorities:

> We were newly-weds. We still walked around holding hands, even if we were just going to the store. I would say to him, 'I love you.' But I didn't know then how much. I had no idea.
>
> We lived in the dormitory of the fire station where he worked. There were three other young couples; we all shared a kitchen. On the ground floor they kept the trucks, the red fire trucks. That was his job.
>
> One night I heard a noise. I looked out the window. He saw me. 'Close the window and go back to sleep. There's a fire at the reactor. I'll be back soon.'

4. Malcolm X, American Civil Rights Leader, (1925–65)

'Let's cool it brothers …'

Spoken to his assassins, three men who shot him 16 times as he delivered a speech at Manhattan's Audabon Ballroom.

5. Indira Gandhi, Prime Minister of India (1917–84)

'I don't mind if my life goes in the service of the nation. If I die today every drop of my blood will invigorate the nation.'

Spoken the night before she was assassinated in New Delhi by her Sikh bodyguards.

6. Karl Marx, German Political Theorist (1818–83)

'Go on, get out – last words are for fools who haven't said enough.'

Spoken to his housekeeper in London, who urged him to tell her his last words so she could write them down for posterity.

>>>

7. Amelia Earhart, American Pilot (1897–1937)

'Please know that I am quite aware of the hazards. Women must try to do things as men have tried. When they fail, their failure must be but a challenge to others.'

From the record-breaking pilot's last letter to her husband before her plane disappeared without trace over New Guinea.

'KHAQQ calling Itasca. We must be on you, but cannot see you. Gas is running low.'

Earhart's last radio communiqué before her disappearance.

8. Joan of Arc, French Saint (c. 1412–31)

'Hold the cross high so I may see it through the flames!'

Spoken as the 19-year-old burned at the stake for heresy.

I didn't see the explosion itself. Just the flames. Everything was radiant. The whole sky. A tall flame. And smoke. The heat was awful. And he's still not back. The smoke was from the burning bitumen, which had covered the roof. He said later it was like walking on tar.

They tried to beat down the flames. They kicked at the burning graphite with their feet ... They weren't wearing their canvas gear. They went off just as they were, in their shirt sleeves. No one told them.

At seven in the morning I was told he was in the hospital. I ran there but the police had already encircled it, and they weren't letting anyone through, only ambulances. The policemen shouted: 'The ambulances are radioactive stay away!'

I saw him. He was all swollen and puffed up. You could barely see his eyes.

'He needs milk. Lots of milk,' my friend said. 'They should drink at least three litres each.'

'But he doesn't like milk.'

'He'll drink it now.'

Many of the doctors and nurses in that hospital, and especially the orderlies, would get sick themselves and die. But we didn't know that then.

I couldn't get into the hospital that evening. The doctor came out and said, yes, they were flying to Moscow, but we needed to bring them their clothes. The clothes they'd worn at the station had been burned off. The buses had stopped running already and we ran across the city. We came running back with their bags, but the plane was already gone. They tricked us.

It was a special hospital, for radiology, and you couldn't get in without a pass. I gave some money to the woman at the door, and she said, 'Go ahead.' Then I had to ask someone else, beg. Finally I'm sitting in the office of the head radiologist. Right away she asked: 'Do you have kids?'

What should I tell her? I can see already that I need to hide that I'm pregnant. They won't let me see him! It's good I'm thin, you can't really tell anything. 'Yes,' I say.

'How many?'

I'm thinking, I need to tell her two. If it's just one, she won't let me in. 'A boy and a girl.'

'So you don't need to have any more. All right, listen: his central nervous system is completely compromised, his skull is completely compromised.'

OK, I'm thinking, so he'll be a little fidgety.

'And listen: if you start crying, I'll kick you out right away. No hugging or kissing. Don't even get near him. You have half an hour.'

He looks so funny, he's got pyjamas on for a size 48, and he's a size 52. The sleeves are too short, the trousers are too short. But his face isn't swollen anymore. They were given some sort of fluid. I say, 'Where'd you run off to?' He wants to hug me. The doctor won't let him. 'Sit, sit,' she says. 'No hugging in here.'

On the very first day in the dormitory they measured me with a dosimeter. My clothes, bag, purse, shoes – they were all 'hot'. And they took that all away from me right there. Even my underwear. The only thing they left was my money.

He started to change; every day I met a brand-new person. The burns started to come to the surface. In his mouth, on his tongue, his cheeks – at first there were little lesions, and then they grew. It came off in layers – as white film ... the colour of his face ... his body ... blue, red, grey-brown. And it's all so very mine.

9. Oscar Wilde, Irish Writer (1854–1900)

'Either that wallpaper goes, or I do.'

Spoken before his death from cerebral meningitis, in self-imposed exile in Paris.

10. Ned Kelly, Australian Folk Hero and Outlaw (1854–80)

'I suppose it had to come to this. Such is life.'

Said as the hangman adjusted the hood to cover his face at Melbourne Gaol.

The only thing that saved me was it happened so fast; there wasn't any time to think, there wasn't any time to cry. It was a hospital for people with serious radiation poisoning. Fourteen days. In 14 days a person dies. He was producing stools 25 to 30 times a day, with blood and mucus. His skin started cracking on his arms and legs. He became covered with boils. When he turned his head, there'd be a clump of hair left on the pillow. I tried joking: 'It's convenient, you don't need a comb.' Soon they cut all their hair.

I tell the nurse: 'He's dying.' And she says to me: 'What did you expect? He got 1,600 roentgen. Four hundred is a lethal dose. You're sitting next to a nuclear reactor.'

When they all died, they refurbished the hospital. They scraped down the walls and dug up the parquet. When he died, they dressed him up in formal wear, with his service cap. They couldn't get shoes on him because his feet had swollen up. They buried him barefoot. My love.

As far as official recognition is concerned, there is very little information. The chief medical officer of the Russian Federation noted in 2001 that 10 per cent of the 184,000 liquidators from Russia had 'died' and one third was 'invalid' or 'sick'. The Ukraine, who provided around 260,000 liquidators said in a press release in April 2005 that 94.2 per cent of them were ill in 2004. The figures are certainly higher now, though it would be dangerous to put an exact figure on them.

Estimates are that 4,000 liquidators from the former Soviet countries still die every year. It is increasingly difficult to locate one of the 800,000 Russian, Byelorussians or

Ukrainians who helped with the close-quarter Chernobyl clean who is not dead or seriously ill.

You can find contradictory information about Chernobyl everywhere, but what is certain is that brave people sacrificed their lives to stem the flow of radiation and died agonisingly, and continue to die, in their thousands.

Gaza Strip Vignette

A firefighter performs the same job all over the world. That is what makes the death of Naji Abu Jalili in Palestine on 6 March 2003 so powerful: this was a man fighting fire in the line of duty who became another war statistic.

Despite being yet another painful reminder of an accident that has been all too commonplace in the Middle East, this is an image that lingers. Directed or misdirected fire from an Israeli tank mowed down the Palestinian fireman as he was clutching a hose. Witnesses told the same story: that a burst of shrapnel from an Israeli tank cut him down. That was what Kemal al-Madhun, the fireman who was standing behind Mr Abu Jalili, said: 'They targeted us, We were about to put the fire out when they shot at us.'

The firemen parked their fire engine in a side street off Jerusalem Street in Jabalya, where they thought it was safe, then took out the hose. Abu Jalili went first, then Madhun, then the driver. 'Naji told me to let go of the hose and let him take it,' said Madhun. 'I turned my back and then the tank fired. If he had not said that, I would have gone forward, it would have been me who died.'

A Day in the Life of ...
Alexandra K. Mosca, an undertaker in Queens County, New York City

'One of the first things you learn in the funeral industry is that there is no typical day. The only constant is death.

Often it's a late-night or early-morning call that begins the day. That insistent ringing of the phone – a phone that is always on and wakes me from sleep – is invariably a 'death call' telling me that somebody has died at home or in a nursing facility which does not have refrigeration. Roused from my slumber, I reach for the pen and pad, which is a permanent fixture on my night stand, to take down preliminary information. I jot down the name of the deceased, the name of the caller and their relationship to the deceased, and the address. I reassure the caller, who is usually a close family member or friend, that my associates will be there as soon as possible to make the removal of the deceased from the home to the funeral home.

As a woman, I do not physically remove bodies from homes – that is the job of the so-called removal men. During the initial telephone conversation, I make an appointment to meet the family for an arrangement conference later in the day, telling the relatives that they can always reach me by telephone if a sudden question arises before we meet.

During my meeting with the family, I go over details of the funeral. It is difficult to see the raw pain, coupled with shock and disbelief, even in cases where a death was anticipated. People want to talk about the death and the deceased, sometimes in great detail. I am a patient listener. It is difficult at times to hear the sad stories of loss and illness. I also find myself thinking about how random, unexpected and unfair life and death can be.

The day of the wake (visitation) is a busy one. Usually in the US wakes will start around 2 p.m. and run until 5 p.m., with evening hours between 7 p.m. and 9 p.m. As funeral directors, we spend the early part of that day dressing the deceased and 'casketing' (carefully arranging the body in the casket in a comfortable-looking position), after which we apply cosmetics and, for females, style hair. As I do this, I sometimes ponder the philosophical questions of life and death. Like the time I was working on a young woman from a photo taken just a few days prior to a flight – a flight which crashed. It was unsettling to see the recent photo of such a lovely and vital young person, now lying in a casket. 'If only she had not taken that flight,' I thought. 'If only' comes to mind a lot. I also wonder to myself, and sometimes out loud to colleagues, whether what we do makes any difference. Is open-casket visitation really a comfort? After all, we can't do what families most want – bring back the dead. We can only ease the transition.

The immediate family usually arrives just before official visiting hours and I walk them into the room, where they will see the deceased in a casket for the first time. After making sure the family is satisfied with how the deceased looks, I go back to my office, returning to the room now and then to see if there is anything they need. To pass the time, I often write or jot notes for articles I am working on. The tone of the wake is different depending upon the age of the deceased and the circumstances of the death. Sometimes I hear laughter coming from the room –it is a social hour for many- other times one can hear a pin drop. I spend the rest of the day in the funeral home, until the evening visitation has ended. During the day, friends will call with social invitations. I always say the same thing, 'I'll have to let you know.'

My experience has been that the least likely thing to happen will and not in a good way. I recall one terribly sad day, being on the phone with one of my closest friends, whose husband was dying from cancer. Call waiting interrupted. On the other end of the phone, another close friend was calling about the sudden death of her husband. What were the chances that my two closest girlfriends would become young widows within months of one another? Even on the peaceful days, a sense of unease is present, as the phone can ring at any time with news of a death.

The night before a funeral, I sometimes have trouble sleeping. I often worry about things that could go wrong but mercifully have not; the hearse breaking down on the way to the cemetery, the pallbearers dropping the casket, the wrong grave being dug. I arise extra early that day, dress in black and meet my hearse driver and the family of the deceased at the funeral home. I am there to direct the events of the day: first the church service, where I lead them down the church aisle, behind the casket, and later at the cemetery for the final committal service. Depending on the season and the weather, cemeteries can be beautiful and serene, a place that makes one feel closer to God, or, on a more wintry, inclement day, like a scary movie set. I stay at the grave until the casket is lowered into the ground. This funeral is over, but before long I will repeat this day with another grieving family. And although it's been a day of sadness and grief, the stark contrast between life and death makes me appreciate all the blessings in my own life. 〟

Noah's Own: Brave Animals

Round the World

Balto

In January 1925 Alaskan doctors realised that a potentially
deadly diphtheria epidemic was poised to sweep through the
city of Nome's population of children; however, the serum
that could stop the outbreak was located in Anchorage, nearly
1,600 kilometres away. The only aircraft that could deliver the
medicine quickly enough was taken out of winter storage;
unfortunately, its engine was frozen, and so the decision was
taken to transport the medicine by sledge. The first part of the
journey was by train, from Anchorage to Nenana, from where
a team of 20 mushers and their dogs were ready to participate
in a relay to take the precious cargo over 1,000 kilometres on
to Nome.

The last leg of the relay was to be led by Norwegian Gunnar
Kaasen and his team. The world's media were watching. His
lead dog, Balto, a Siberian husky, was a relative rookie
compared to the other animals, but it was up to him to lead
Kaasen and the life-saving remedy the final 85 kilometres.

As soon as they set off they hit terrible conditions, including
strong winds and a blizzard. Kaasen could barely see a mere
metre ahead. It was all down to Balto, whose navigational
instincts took over. The dog saved his team from certain death
in the Topkok river when he refused to go on because the ice
was cracking, and he managed to keep them on the trail in a
terrible white-out. It took Kaasen's team 20 hours to complete
their heroic mission. They arrived at
Nome at 5.30 a.m. on 2 February with
the dogs too tired and weak to bark. The
serum was administered in the nick of
time. Balto and his team, and all the other
mushers and their dogs, shot to worldwide fame

for preventing an epidemic and saving so many lives. The run is commemorated by the annual Iditarod Trail Sledge Dog Race.

Follow the Bear

Wojtek – dubbed the 'Soldier Bear' – was rescued in the Middle East in 1943 and adopted by Polish troops when he was a cub. They nursed him from empty vodka bottles filled with condensed milk. When the Polish forces were deployed in Italy, they enlisted the bear as a solder, which allowed him to be taken with them. So, this Syrian brown bear was given a name, a rank and a serial number and took part in the Italian campaign. As he grew he was trained to carry heavy-mortar rounds for the Polish troops and saw action on the front line at the Battle of Monte Cassino.

He grew so tame he could be trusted with children and he even learned to drink beer and smoke, though he had an unruly habit of eating the cigarettes. He also learned how to work the troops' showers, but he loved cooling off so much that the soldiers had to lock the shower to prevent him using up all of the water.

After the war he lived at an army camp in the Scottish Borders before ending his days at Edinburgh Zoo. Efforts are now being made by the Wojtek Memorial Trust to build a permanent tribute to the bear.

Doctor Kanga

A one-eyed pet kangaroo called Lulu saved a farmer's life in Australia by alerting his family that he was unconscious. Leonard Richards had been knocked out by a tree branch in April 2004 while out and about with Lulu, whom they had adopted when she was young because she was blind in one eye. A wise decision. The clever kangaroo, sensing that all was not right, bounded back to the farmer's home in Victoria and banged on the door, barking, until his wife came out to see what was wrong. She followed Lulu to her husband, who would have died if he hadn't received urgent medical attention.

Dieting Pig

One of the most famous animals in the People's Republic of China is a hardy pig that somehow survived for 36 days buried beneath rubble after the earthquake in Sichuan in 2008. The pig lived on rainwater and a bag of charcoal for over a month and, having lost two thirds of his body weight, looked more like a goat than a swine when he was found. The pig, whose name is Zhu Jianqiang (meaning 'Strong Pig'), has since won the Chinese Animal of the Year award. Zhu has also been used as an example of the nation's resilience in a tough economic climate. On a warming personal note for this snouty celebrity, the pig himself earned a get-out-of-jail card from the slaughterhouse and now leads a cushy life as the top attraction at an earthquake museum. He continues to eat himself into contented obesity.

Dolphin Escort

In August 2007, Todd Endris was attacked by a Great White shark while out surfing off the Californian coast. The four-and-a-half-metre maneater emerged suddenly from the depths – Endris had not been aware of its approach until its jaws were upon him. The vice-like grip peeled the skin off Endris's back and then the shark mauled his leg to the bone. But just when Endris thought his struggle was over, and after a third munch when the shark tried to swallow his leg, a pod of bottlenose dolphins suddenly appeared and intervened. They kept the shark at bay and formed a protective ring around Endris. He then wriggled clear, with the dolphins encircling him as he managed to paddle on his surfboard back to shore, where first aid provided by a friend also helped to save his life.

Unsinkable Sam

This unfortunate German feline, landlubber though he may have been, became the most famous mascot of the British Royal Navy. The black-and-white-patched cat had been owned by an unknown crewman of the German battleship *Bismarck*. He was aboard ship on 18 May 1941 when it set sail on Operation Rheinubung, *Bismarck*'s first and only mission. It was sunk in a battle just over a week later, with only 115 survivors from its crew of over 2,200. Hours later, a bedraggled cat was found floating on a board and picked from the water, the only survivor to be rescued by the British destroyer HMS *Cossack*. Unaware of his name, the crew of *Cossack* named their new mascot Oscar.

He served on board for the next few months as the ship carried out duties in the Mediterranean and North Atlantic. On 24 October 1941, *Cossack* was escorting a convoy from Gibraltar to the UK when it was severely damaged by a torpedo fired by a German U-boat. The explosion killed 159 of the crew but Oscar survived again and was transferred to the Gibraltar shore before the boat sank.

Now nicknamed 'Unsinkable Sam' he was put aboard HMS *Ark Royal*, an aircraft carrier that had been instrumental in the destruction of Oscar's first floating home. However, the *Ark Royal* was torpedoed on its way back from Malta in 1941 by another U-boat and the carrier slowly rolled over and sank.

Ten Trusty Steeds

1. Pegasus

In Greek mythology Pegasus was a wild winged horse, eventually tamed by the daring Bellerophon. With Pegasus as his flying mount, Bellerophon slayed the dreaded beast known as Chimera. Pegasus has remained a fairy-story favourite.

2. Bucephalus

Alexander the Great tamed this wild horse by turning its head into the sun, thereby preventing it from being frightened by its own shadow. Bucephalus then became Alexander's mount for many of his military campaigns. The horse was eventually killed in battle and given a solemn funeral by Alexander himself.

3. Babieca

In eleventh-century Spain, the monk Pedro El Grande offered his godson Rodrigo Diaz de Bivar the pick of a herd of beautiful Andalusian horses. Rodrigo chose a white foal he named Babieca, or 'my stupid one'. This white stallion carried Rodrigo, better known as El Cid to the Saracens, into battle for 30 years, and every time to victory. After the death of El Cid in the battle for Valencia, Babieca never carried a mount again and died two years later at the ripe old age of 40.

4. Matsukaze

Matsukaze means 'wind in the pines'. No one could tame this wild horse until the samurai Maeda Toshimasu (1543–1612), who was just as wild, finally met him. The two became inseparable. Matsukaze was a monumental horse, formidably strong, able to carry his master's huge bulk for days. After Toshimasu's death, Matsukaze ran off and was never seen again.

5. Chetak

The noble war horse of Rana Pratap of Mewar in India is still famous in Indian folk legend. The horse was a Marwari breed and Pratap was mounted on Chetak in the gruesome battle of Haldighati (1576), in which the horse gave up his life to save his master.

6. Black Bess

Black Bess was the trusty steed of the legendary eighteenth-century English highwayman Dick Turpin. The story was that he stole her at gunpoint from a man named Mr Major and that she was better bred than her rapscallion owner.

7. Nelson

The first president of the United States, George Washington, had a horse called Nelson who carried him through his most important battles: Valley Forge and Yorktown. Washington was also riding Nelson when the British surrendered.

8. Marengo

Named after the Battle of Marengo, this grey Arabian horse was Napoleon's most reliable, steady and courageous mount. Marengo was wounded eight times in his career, and carried the Emperor in the battles of Austerlitz, Jena-Auerstedt, Wagram and, finally, Waterloo, where here he was captured and taken back to England in 1815.

9. Comanche

At the Battle of Little Big Horn in 1876, which was famously the last stand of General George Custer, the only survivor was the horse of Captain Miles Keogh.

Comanche was found on the battlefield three days after the fight with arrows still sticking to his body. He was taken to Bismarck and nursed back to health. As a reward for his bravery he was only used in parades for the rest of his life.

10. Arkle

This Irish racehorse was the dream steeplechase steed for any jockey and was a thoroughbred in a league of his own when it came to jumping fences. He won three consecutive Cheltenham Gold Cups (1964, 1965, 1966) and became a legendary hero in Ireland. His strength was jokingly claimed to come from drinking Guinness.

A long-suffering Sam was found clinging to another floating plank by a rescue launch, looking 'angry but unharmed'. Much to his feline relief, the sinking of the *Royal* was the end of Sam's naval career and he was transferred first to the offices of the governor of Gibraltar, and then sent back to the UK, where he saw out the remainder of the war living in a home for seamen in Belfast. Sam died in 1955.

Dogs of War

Man's best friend has been at our side since the dawn of time. Egyptian wall writings dating back to 4000 BC depict savage dogs on leads held by Egyptian warriors, leaping on their enemies. From mastiffs in chain mail to the anti-tank dogs at Stalingrad, dogs have proved invaluable in warfare, exploited by man for their loyalty, and have bled and died for their countries like the toughest of soldiers.

Mastiffs

The Romans used giant mastiffs, huge ancestors of the Roman Rottweiler, to fight in battle in the first and second centuries. The Romans had attack formations made up entirely of dogs, who were also used to herd and protect cattle when the Romans were travelling.

Attila the Hun used a pack of huge Molosser dogs (a giant early breed of mastiff) to stand as sentries around his camps, so as not to be surprised by his enemies during his war campaigns in fifth-century Europe.

In 1518, King Henry VIII of England presented 400 battle mastiffs with iron collars to Charles V of Spain, who was at war with France. The mastiffs were set on the French dogs at the Siege of Valencia and drove them from the battlefield with their proverbial tails between their legs. The English dogs were commended by Charles and held up as an example to his troops.

In the fifteenth century, snarling mastiffs and greyhounds were used by the Spanish to hunt down men and fight in the conquests of the Indians of Mexico and Peru. 'Tomalo', roughly translated as 'go get them', was the command for the dogs to attack.

Poodles

In 1642, Prince Rupert was appointed by King Charles to lead the Royalist cavalry during the English Civil War. He was known as the 'Mad Cavalier' and was accompanied by his white poodle Boye when he rode into battle. Throughout the war the Parliamentarians feared this dog, claiming it slept in Rupert's bed, was fed on the choicest morsels of roast beef and had supernatural powers. Boye was Prince Rupert's constant companion until the dog's death at the Battle of Marston Moor in 1644.

Perhaps the most famous of all the poodles that went to war was the Napoleonic army's Moustache, a black poodle who rescued the regimental standard at the Battle of Austerlitz by dragging it away from an Austrian soldier and bringing it back to the French. He even performed various tricks, most famously lifting his leg at the mention of the Emperor's enemies. He was later killed at the storming of Badajoz and was buried with full military honours.

'After the Battle of Marengo,' Napoleon wrote in

Tireless Jock Spider

A small unnamed arachnid was the inspiration behind one of the greatest victories in the history of Scotland. In the fourteenth century, Robert the Bruce lay freezing in a cave, demoralised by his abortive efforts to defeat the English. As he lay on his straw bed he spotted a spider hanging by a thin filament, desperately trying to weave its web. Six times he watched it fail to fasten this thread; nevertheless, it kept trying.

Bruce decided that if the spider succeeded on its seventh go he himself would try again to fight the English. The spider triumphed and Bruce leaped up, threw off his despair and defeated the English at Bannockburn in 1314. The rest of the spider's life is not documented.

Glow-Worms

Although not all of them may have willingly volunteered for the role, the use of glow-worms was indispensable in the trenches of France and Belgium in the First World War. Their light was used by soldiers to read maps in the darkness.

his memoirs, 'I walked over the battlefield and saw among the slain a poodle killed, bestowing a last lick upon his dead friend's face. Never had anything on any of my battlefields caused me a like emotion.'

German War-Dog School

In 1884, the German Army established the first military dog-training school at Lechenich, near Berlin, where they pioneered methods of preparing dogs to be sentries and messengers. Various breeds of gun dogs were first used, along with poodles, Airedales, farm collies, German shepherds and Dobermanns. The German shepherd was especially favoured because of its ability to understand commands, its endurance, watchfulness and readiness. Only pure-breds were accepted for service and the most careful precautions were taken to prevent cross-breeding.

Puppies' tails were docked by the time they were four weeks old, with instruction beginning in their seventh month by exercising them on a lead. No barking was permitted, and no dog was allowed to develop a taste for hunting, or for game.

A year later, in 1885, the school published the first manuals for training war dogs. The handbook clearly indicated that the Imperial German Army had fully accepted the use of dogs in warfare. The tables of organisation for Jaeger battalions showed at least two dogs assigned to a company, with a maximum of twelve to a full battalion.

It was emphasised that only men who had genuine love for the animals would be accepted into the dog-training programme: 'on this essentially the animal's performance depends ... the efficacy of a dog heavily depends on the choice of its attendants and the special instructions. Faulty treatment will lessen the efficiency of the animal; special attention also must be given to its kennelling and, if necessary, its cleaning and drying.'

The Germans were also the first to introduce the Red Cross dog units – with animals equipped with saddlebags containing medical supplies, to search and find the wounded on a field of battle.

In the First World War the Germans' well-trained dogs gave them an advantage over the Allies and they saved many men's lives by padding round the trenches delivering vital messages.

Kamikaze Dogs

The Eastern front in Russia in the Second World War was desperately brutal. The Russians, particularly at Stalingrad, used whatever means possible to repel the Germans. One method they developed was the use of canine suicide bombers. The dogs were kept hungry so that they would search for food placed beneath tanks during training. Once on the battlefield they were fitted with a box of explosives and then released before oncoming German tanks. When the dog dived under them, a wooden lever sticking up from the top of box was tripped and the charge detonated. Things didn't always go according to plan, though. The Russians used their own diesel tanks for training, which meant on the battlefield the hungry dogs sometimes sought out their own tanks rather than the enemy's. Otherwise, the anti-tank dogs were hugely successful and the Germans were compelled to take measures against them. But the animals were speedy, low to the ground and tricky to spot, thus difficult to deter or eliminate. Eventually the Germans used tank-mounted flame-throwers to ward off the attacks. In German, the dogs were called *Hundminen* (meaning 'dog-mines') and destroyed in the region of 300 of their tanks.

German Guard Rat

Rats may not be everyone's cup of tea, but they can be sharp, brave, intelligent creatures. The Steich family in Stuttgart were protected by their pet rat when armed burglars broke into their home one night. The diminutive rodent, named Gerd, launched his attack from a hiding place in the bookcase, managing to land his teeth on the face of one burglar before he fell ravenously on the foot of the other and scurried up his trouser leg. The robbery was averted.

Winged Saviour

A heroic pigeon saved the lives of 11 aircrew in the Second World War. An RAF Catalina flying boat had to ditch in the Hebrides in October 2003 and sea-rescue operations were hindered by very bad weather. Their only hope was a pigeon called White Vision, who flew nearly 100 kilometres into a 40-kilometre-per-hour headwind and delivered a message. As a result the search was resumed, the aircraft sighted and the crew rescued.

>>>

George, a Jack Russell terrier from New Zealand, sacrificed his life to save a group of children from being mauled by two pit bulls in 2007. George fought with the pit bulls in the North Island town of Manaia to keep them from attacking five children as they returned home from buying sweets at a local shop. George was so badly mauled in the melee that he was later put down. American war veteran Jerrell Hudman has since immortalised George by sending him one of the Purple Heart medals he was awarded in Vietnam.

Yankee Mutts

SERGEANT STUBBY

This little brute is the most decorated dog in US military history. As a small stray bull terrier, Stubby was smuggled aboard a troop ship to France, where he worked alongside the soliders of the 102nd Infantry in the trenches of the Western Front. He recovered to serve in battles at Château-Thierry, the Marne and the Meuse-Argonne. Since he could hear the whine of incoming artillery shells before humans could, he became adept at alerting his unit to the oncoming bombardment.

One night in February 1918 he roused a sleeping sergeant just before the onset of a gas attack. The warning gave the soldiers time to don masks and saved their lives. He was also solely responsible for capturing a German spy in the Argonne, and he learned to approximate a salute with his paw. He was given life membership in the American Legion and the Red Cross; he met Presidents Wilson, Harding and Coolidge and died of old age in 1926.

CHIPS

A mongrel mix of German shepherd, collie and husky, Chips was suicidally brave. When he and his handler were attacked in an ambush in July 1943 during the invasion of Sicily, he streaked over to the Italian machine-gun pillbox to capture four Italian soldiers and save his handler. He suffered powder burns and a scalp wound – proof that the Italians had tried to kill him. That same night he helped capture another 10 soldiers. Chips was personally thanked for his services by General Eisenhower.

Nemo

Airman Bob Thorneburg and his German shepherd Nemo were assigned patrol duty near an old Vietnamese graveyard in 1966. Nemo alerted them to the presence of another person in the cemetery. Then someone opened fire.

Thorneburg released his dog and charged, firing in the direction of the enemy. Nemo was wounded when a bullet entered just under his right eye and exited through his mouth. Thorneburg killed one Viet Cong before he too was shot in the shoulder and knocked to the ground. Then Nemo, with his face blown apart, managed to get up and throw himself ferociously on the remaining guerrillas. His attack bought Thorneburg the time he needed to call in backup forces. Nemo then crawled to his master and covered him with his body. Even after help arrived, Nemo would not allow anyone to touch Thorneburg. The backup found four more Viet Cong hiding underground.

Thorneburg fully recovered from his injuries and returned home with honours. It required many skin grafts to restore Nemo's appearance, and he too was retired from duty and returned to the United States as a war hero.

Para Pups

Dogs were first trained to parachute during the Second World War and were used on scouting missions for the Allied troops or to keep watch over tired soldiers. The British were the first to train the dogs to be dropped with SAS regiments or transport messages behind enemy lines.

A working farm dog – a collie called Rob – became one of the first 'para pups'. He watched over and protected the exhausted men and played a vital role in being parachuted in behind enemy lines with his SAS unit. He made over 20 descents during his time with various units in North Africa and Italy. Brian, another German shepherd, took part in the D-Day landings as a patrol dog attached to a parachute battalion. He landed in Normandy and later, based on his number of successful jumps, became a fully qualified paratrooper. Both animals received the prestigious Dickin Medal, the animal equivalent of the Victoria Cross.

Scout dogs were also used during the Second World War by the US Marine Corps, who began to train dogs in 1942. A German shepherd called, rather flouncily, Jaint de Mortimorney, completed more jumps than any US soldier in the war and was an indispensable watchdog on operations in France. He even wore the paratrooper insignia on his flanks.

US paratroopers did, however, once use an untrained Dobermann, whom they unceremoniously kicked out of a plane, albeit with a special parachute. After landing in the midst of his fellow US troops the dog started to growl at his own men, much to their annoyance, until a few minutes later four Germans appeared – the Dobermann had been doing his job as a watchdog.

Para pups are still in service but now jump from higher altitudes. The elite American unit Delta Force has pioneered the canine parachute technique called 'High Altitude High Opening' as part of the War on Terror. In the UK German shepherds are being trained to jump from aircraft at 7,600 metres, drifting up to 30 kilometres towards their target. They are strapped to members of SAS assault teams, with their own oxygen masks full of dog breath. With tiny cameras fixed to their heads, the animals will be able to scout ahead to hunt for insurgent hideouts in Afghanistan, beaming live images back to the SAS troops as they penetrate enemy lines. It is hoped the technique will reduce the level of danger to the coalition special-forces units, even though some of the dogs may suffer in the line of duty.

British Bomb Squad

Buster, a springer spaniel with the Royal Army Veterinary Corps, broke a resistance cell in Safwan, southern Iraq, in April 2003, when he sniffed out a secret cache of arms and explosives. Led by his handler, Sergeant Danny Morgan, Buster's sensitive snout delved into a wall cavity behind a wardrobe and then under a sheet of tin. The stash included AK-47 assault rifles, a pistol, grenades, ammunition and bomb-making equipment and led to the arrest of 16 pro-Saddam Hussein supporters.

Sadie, a black Labrador whose speciality is the search for explosives, is another member of the Royal Veterinary Corps. She became an instant hero when she sniffed out a terrorist bomb in Kabul in November 2005. The device, hidden in a pressure cooker, had been planted under sandbags metres from where a suicide car bombing had killed a German soldier. Over 200 people, including British, American and Greek soldiers, were within range of the device. Sadie and her handler, Lance-Corporal Karen Yardley, had been called to check for secondary devices after the initial explosion. The booby trap was discovered after Sadie's tail wagged vigorously. She sniffed the air, then her tail went rigid and she sat down facing the wall. The device was found quickly and bomb-disposal experts arrived and used a remote-controlled robot to defuse the device. Sadie, who is now retired, was later awarded the Dickin Medal.

Bear – China: male symbol of strength and bravery.

Boar – Ancient Celts: in addition to representing fertility and wealth, boars symbolise courage and strength.

Carp – Japan: since it swims upstream, undeterred even by rapids, the carp symbolises courage, perseverance and transformation.

Cougar – Native American Indians: leadership, courage, power, swiftness and balance.

Crab – Ancient Greece: Hera placed the crab in the heavens because it had the courage to bite Hercules' heel while he was struggling with the Hydra.

Cricket – China: associated with summer, resurrection (due to their emergence from the larval stage), courage, happiness and good luck.

Eagle – Native American Indians: bravery, acuity and strength.

Animal Symbols of Bravery: Medieval Heraldry

Heraldry blossomed in the Middle Ages as a means of recognising warriors on the battlefield. By the middle of the twelfth century, knights were wearing full protective body armour and helmets which made them difficult to tell apart, so to identify themselves these warriors decorated their shields. Colour was used first as a means of telling friend from foe, but soon knights used symbols, called 'charges', to denote their personality and accomplishments. Charges were usually objects taken from nature, and each was ascribed a special meaning. They often formed the knight's crest, which he wore emblazoned on his helmet, so that he could be more easily spotted at a distance on the battlefield.

Heraldry has been coined 'the shorthand of history', with coats of arms registered over the centuries to denote family or civil records. The word 'heraldry' goes back to the days of jousting, when the herald would trumpet his knight's arrival and wow the crowd with his feats of valour. The use of animal imagery is one of the oldest forms of symbolism, and the most popular. Here is a list of some of those animals used in medieval heraldry and what they symbolised:

Badger: bravery, perseverance and protection.

Bagwyn *(a heraldic beast with the body and tail of a horse, and with long horns curved over the ears)*: fierceness and bravery in defence of king and country.

Boar: bravery; fights to the death.

Bull/Buffalo: valour, bravery and generosity.

Cat *(also Wildcat/Lynx)*: liberty, vigilance, forecast and courage.

Cock: courage and perseverance; a hero; politically savvy.

Dog/Talbot: courage, vigilance and loyalty.

Dragon: a defender of treasure; valour and protection.

Eagle: Nobility, strength, bravery and alertness.

Elephant: strength and stature, wisdom, courage, longevity, happiness, royalty, good luck, and ambition.

Griffin: valour and death-defying bravery; vigilance.

Hippogriff (*half horse, half eagle*): bravery protecting one's home and family.

Leopard: a valiant and hardy warrior who enterprises hazardous things by force and courage.

Lion: dauntless courage, bravery, strength, ferocity and valour.

Ox: valour and generosity.

Paschal lamb: faith, innocence, bravery, gentleness, purity and resolute spirit.

Sea Lion: dauntless courage at sea.

Tiger: fierceness and valour, resentment; dangerous if aroused.

Unicorn: extreme courage, virtue and strength.

Wyvern (*a winged reptilian creature with two legs*): valour and protection.

Ermine – Inuit: especially honoured because of its quickness and courage, despite its small size. Ermine skins were thought to protect women.

Jaguar – Aztec & Mayan civilisations: thought to be the alter-ego of high and powerful shamen.

Rabbit – Native American Indians: symbolises the conquering of fear.

Tiger – Chinese Astrology: loyal, courageous, energetic, strong and cunning.

Read More About It

War

Amitai-Preiss, Reuven, *Mongols and Mamluks: The Mamluk–Ilkhanid War, 1260–1281*, Cambridge University Press, 1995.

Belich, James, *The New Zealand Wars*, Penguin Books Australia Ltd, 1998.

Cornelius H Charlton entry, Medal of Honor Recipient: Korean War. Center of Military History, United States Army, 16 July 2007.

Gergel, Tania, ed., *Alexander the Great: The Brief Life and Towering Exploits of History's Greatest Conqueror As Told by His Original Biographers*, Penguin, 2004.

Haukelid, Knut, *Skis Against the Atom: The Exciting, First Hand Account of Heroism and Daring Sabotage During the Nazi Occupation of Norway*, North American Heritage Press, 1989.

Kahn, Paul and Woodman Cleaves, Francis, *The Secret History of the Mongols: The Origin of Chingis Khan*, C & T Asian Culture Series, 1998.

Kurzman, Dan, *Blood and Water: Sabotaging Hitler's Bomb*, Henry Holt and Co, 1997.

Scott-Kilvert, Ian, *The Age of Alexander*, Penguin Classics, 1973.

Wiggan, Richard, *Operation Freshman: The Rjukan Heavy Water Raid 1942*, William Kimber and Co, Ltd, 1986.

High Seas

Ferreras, Pippin, *The Dive: A Tale of Love and Obsession*, William Morrow, 2004.

Goddard, Jacqui, 'Deep, deep breath gives world dive record to "mermaid" who overcame her fear of the sea', *The Times*, 3 April 2009.

Graham, Thomas, *Pirate Hunter: the Life of Captain Woodes Rogers*, Pen & Sword Maritime, 2008.

Levathes, Louise, *When China Ruled the Seas*, reprinted by Oxford University Press, 1996.

McCarthy, Terry and DeQuine, Jeanne, 'In Miami and Tala Skari in Paris, Lost in the Big Blue', *Time* magazine, 18 November 2002.

Morrison, JS, Coates, JF and Rankov, NB, *The Athenian Trireme: The History and Reconstruction of an Ancient Greek Trireme*, Cambridge University Press; 2nd ed., 2000.

Shirer, William L, *Berlin Diary: The Journal of a Foreign Correspondent, 1934–41*, Johns Hopkins University Press, 2002.

Tweddle, Dominic and Hall, Richard, *Viking Ships*, Cultural Resource Management Ltd, York Archaeological Trust, 1987.

Wilson, Alexander, *No Purchase, No Pay – Morgan, Kidd and Woodes Rogers in the Great Age of Privateers and Pirates 1665–1715*, Eyre & Spottiswoode, 1970.

Aviation

Collis, Maurice, *Into Hidden Burma*, Faber & Faber, 1953.

Hart, Clive, *The Prehistory of Flight*, University of California Press, 1985.

Hoffman, Paul, *Wings of Madness: Alberto Santos-Dumont and the Invention of Flight*, Hyperin Press, 2003.

Kittinger, Joseph, *The Long Lonely Leap*, Dutton, 1961.

Markham, Beryl, *West with the Night*, North Point Press, 1942 (reprint 1983).

Pennington, Reina, *Wings, Women, and War: Soviet Airwomen in WWII Combat*, University Press of Kansas, 1997.

Piszkiewicz, Dennis, *The Fantastic Flights of Hanna Reitsch*, Praeger, 1997.

Reitsch, Hanna, *The Sky My Kingdom*, Greenhill Books, 1997.

Riviera, Ray, 'Pilot Becomes a Hero in the Making', *New York Times*, 15 January 2009.

Russell Coulter, Charles and Turner, Patricia, *Dictionary of Ancient Deities*, Oxford University Press Inc, 2001.

Wheeler, Sara, *Too Close to the Sun: The Audacious Life and Times of Denys Finch Hatton*, Random House, 2006.

Samurai

Cohen, Richard, *Sword*, Random House, 2002.

McCullough, Helen, *Tale of the Heike*, Stamford University Press, 1st ed., 2000.

Milton, Giles, *Samurai William: The Englishman Who Opened the East*, Farrar, Straus and Giroux, 2003.

Sakai, Saboro, Martin Caiden: *Samurai!*, I Books, 2001.

Turnbull, Stephen, *The Samurai Sourcebook*, Cassell, 2000.

Turnbull, Stephen, *Warriors of Medieval Japan*, Osprey Publishing, 2005.

William Adams's letter, 1612.

Yanamoto, Tsunetomo, *Hagakure: The Book of the Samurai*, tr. William Scott Wilson, Kodansha International, 1992.

Survival

Armstrong, Lance, *It's Not About the Bike: My Journey Back to Life*, Yellow Jersey Press, 2001.

Danner, Mark, *The Massacre of El Mozote*, Vintage, 1994.

Howarth, David, *We Die Alone*, The Lyons Press, 2007.

Lum McCunn, Ruthanne, *Sole Survivor: A Story of Record Endurance at Sea*, Beacon Press, 1999.

Martin, Douglas, 'Rufina Amaya, 64, dies; Salvador Survivor', *New York Times*, 9 March 2007.

McKale, Donald M, *Hitler: The Survival Myth*, Cooper Square Press, 2001.

Megee, Ricky, *Left for Dead in the Outback*, Nicholas Brealey Publishing, 2008.

Morgan, Ted, 'The Barbie File', *New York Times* magazine, 10 May 1987.

Ralston, Aron, *Between a Rock and a Hard Place*, Atria Books, 2004.

Rawicz, Slavomir, *The Long Walk*, The Lyons Press, 1997.

Espionage, Regimes & Revolutionaries

Bar-Zohar, Michael, *The Most Extraordinary True Spy Story of World War II*, Macmillan Publishing Company, 1985.

Bloch, Michael, *The Duchess of Windsor*, Weidenfeld & Nicolson. 1996.

Conboy, Kenneth and Morrison, James, *The CIA's Secret War in Tibet*, University Press of Kansas, 2002.

Guevara, Ernesto 'Che', *Guerrilla Warfare*, www.bnpublishing.com, 1997.

King, Greg, *The Duchess of Windsor; The Uncommon Life of Wallis Simpson*, Citadel Press, 2001.

Lee Anderson, Jon, *Che Guevara: A Revolutionary Life*, Bantam Books, 1997.

LeGates, Marlene, *In Their Time*, Routledge, 2001.

Plutarch, *Plutarch: Life of Antony*, ed. C B R Pelling, Cambridge University Press, 2008.

Raybin Emert, Phyllis, ed., *Women in the Civil War*, History Compass, 2007.

Renshon, Stanley A, *National Security in the Obama Administration*, Routledge, 2009.

Stephens, Winifred, *Women of the French Revolution*, Kessinger Publishing, 2005.

United States Secret Service website: www.secretservice.gov

Walker, Susan and Higgs, Peter, eds., *Cleopatra of Egypt*, Princeton University Press, 2001.

The White House website: www.whitehouse.gov

Exploration

Butcher, Tim, *Blood River: A Journey to Africa's Broken Heart*, Vintage, 2007.

Dugard, Martin, *Into Africa: The Epic Adventures of Stanley and Livingstone*, Bantam Books, 2004.

Greenfield, Susan, 'What brain science will do to all our futures', *Independent*, 21 January 2002.

Greenfield, Susan, *The Private Life of the Brain*, Penguin, 2002.

Hendrickson, Sue, *Hunt for the Past: My Life as an Explorer*, Scholastic Inc., 2001.

Horn, Mike, www.mikehorn.com

Humphreys, Alastair, *Moods of Future Joys*, Adlibbed Ltd, 2006.

Humphreys, Alastair, *Thunder and Sunshine*, Eye Books, 2007.

Lewis, Jon E, ed., *The Mammoth Book of On the Edge*, Running Press, 2009.

Mee, Margaret, *Margaret Mee's Amazon: The Diaries of an Artist Explorer*, Antique Collectors' Club Ltd, 2004.

Rupke, Nicolaas A, *Alexander von Humboldt, A Metabiography*, Chicago University Press, 2008.

The Language of Bravery

Ayto, John, ed., *Brewer's Dictionary of Phrase and Fable*, 17th rev. ed., Weidenfeld & Nicolson, 2007.

Barnhart, Robert K, *Chambers Dictionary of Etymology*, Chambers Harrap, 1999.

Fitzhenry, Robert I, *The Harper Book of Quotations*, 3rd ed., Collins, 1993.

Stone, John R, *The Routledge World Book of Proverbs*, new ed., Routledge, 2006.

Sport

Askwith, Richard, *Feet in the Clouds: A Story of Fell-Running and Obsession*, Aurum Press, 2005.

Harris, Harry, *Pelé: His Life and Times*, Parkwest, 2002.

Henry, Marguerite, *The Palio: The Wildest Horse Race in the World*, Armada Books, 1977.

Jordan, Tom, *Pre: The Story of America's Greatest Running Legend, Steve Prefontaine*, Rodale Press, 1998.

Marantz, Steve, *Sorcery at Caesars: Sugar Ray's Marvelous Fight*, Inkwater Press, 2008.

Pelé, *My Life and the Beautiful Game*, Doubleday, 1977.

Stefanello, Vinicio, 'Alexander Odintsov: Jannu Expedition Leader', tr. Betta Gobbi, www.planetmountain.com

Escape

Apthorpe, Graham, *A Town at War*, Cowra Local Press, 2008.

Charrière, Henri, *Papillon*, tr. by Patrick O'Brian, HarperCollins, 1994.

Clinton, Catherine, *Harriet Tubman: The Road to Freedom*, Little, Brown and Company, 2004.

Dengler, Dieter, *Escape from Laos*, Presido Press, 1979.

Eastman, Charles A, *Indian Heroes and Great Chieftains*, Dodo Press, 2007.

Foot, MRD, and Langley, JM, *MI9*, Little, Brown and Company, 1980.

Hayes, Paddy, *Break-out!: Famous Prison Escapes*, O'Brien Press, 2004.

Neave, Airey, *Saturday at MI9: The Classic Account of the World War Two Allied Escape Organisation*, Leo Cooper, 2003.

Wetzler, Alfred, *Escape from Hell: The Story of Auschwitz Protocol*, Berghahn Books, 2003.

Wade, Cecil W, *Symbolisms of Heraldry*, Kessinger Publishing, 2003.

Werness, Hope B, *The Continuum Encyclopedia of Animal Symbolism in Art*, Continuum, 2006.

Zaloga, Steve, *The Red Army of the Great Patriotic War, 1941–45*, Osprey Publishing, 1989.

Death

Alexievich, Svetlana, *Voices from Chernobyl: The Oral History of a Nuclear Disaster*, tr. Keith Gessen, Picador, 2006.

The Captain Patrick J. Brown Memorial Foundation www.captpatrickbrown.org.

Engel, Howard, *Lord High Executioner: An Unashamed Look at Hangmen, Headsmen, and Their Kind*, Key Porter Books, 1996.

Huggler, Justin, 'Indelible image of Palestinian fireman killed by shrapnel', *Independent*, 8 March, 2003.

Jenkins, Sally, 'Company of Heroes', *Washington Post*, 20 September, 2001.

Kohne, Eckart and Ewigleben, Cornelian, *Gladiators and Caesars*, British Museum Press, 2000.

Lenotre, Gilles, *La Guillotine pendant la Revolution*, Perrin, 1893.

Wiedemann, Thomas, *Emperors and Gladiators*, Routledge, 1992.

Noah's Own

Chongqing Evening Post, China, 22 June 2008.

Fox-Davies, Arthur Charles and Johnston, Graham, *A Complete Guide to Heraldry*, Kessinger Publishing, 2004.

Hamer, Blythe, *Dogs at War: True Stories of Canine Courage Under Fire*, Andre Deutsch, 2006.

Lernish, Michael G, *War Dogs: A History of Loyalty and Heroism*, Potomac, 1999.

Lewis, Val, *Ships' Cats in War and Peace*, Nauticalia, 2001.

Sydney Morning Herald, 22 September 2003.

Acknowledgements

I'd like to thank the following people and organisations for their help with *The Bumper Book of Bravery*: Baroness Susan Greenfield; Lance Corporal Matthew Croucher; The Royal Navy; Michael Thornton; Sam Davies; The Royal Air Force; Neil Laughton; Giles Cardozo; Charlie Bell; Federal Aviation Administration; Bob Stuart; the CIA Archives; Alexandra Mosca; Andy Whittaker; the Foreign and Commonwealth Office; Mike and Cathy Horn; Meg Ford; Alastair Humphreys; Patrick Truman; Jane and Oliver Grieve; Dr Ian Fairlie; The City of New York Fire Department; Mark Hartell; The Tibetan Tourist Board; Shane Williams; Peter Owen; Tristan McConnell; Mama Muliri; the PDSA; Sarah MacGregor; Breck; Rufus; Hugo.

I'd also like to thank all those at Virgin including Louisa Joyner, Kelly Falconer, Sophia Brown and Toby Clarke; the designer Lindsay Nash and the illustrator Nicole Heidaripour; also Helen Szirtes and Hugo de Klee; my agent Charlie Campbell at Ed Victor; Kitson, for putting up with me disappearing from best-man duty; little George Quick and bigger Ed Richardson; Lesley Herd; the Nobla; Mark Bevan; and Rags, who deserves a medal of her own for putting up with my whirring head.